ENGLISH ⬚ HERITAGE

Book of
Ships and Shipwrecks

ENGLISH ❖ HERITAGE

Book of
Ships and Shipwrecks

Peter Marsden

B. T. Batsford Ltd / English Heritage
London

© Peter Marsden 1997

First published 1997

Typeset by Bernard Cavender Design & Greenwood Graphics Publishing
Printed and bound in Great Britain by The Bath Press, Bath

Published by B.T. Batsford Ltd
583 Fulham Road, London SW6 5BY

A CIP catalogue record for this book is
available from the British Library

ISBN 0 7134 7535 8 (cased)
0 7134 7536 6 (limp)

(Front cover) Wreck of the *Anne* visible at low tide.

(Back cover) The bow of a reconstructed Viking ship
preserved at Ramsgate.

Contents

Illustrations

Colour plates

Between pages 64 and 65

Preface and acknowledgements

One cannot read any book about the historical or archaeological heritage of Britain without meeting evidence of its maritime past, be it imported trade goods, warfare or migrations of peoples. This is taken for granted, but for a long time the evidence of the ships and ports involved in those events has been placed on the edge of mainstream research, with the result that maritime archaeology has for over a century been treated as a 'new' or specialist subject. As very few people were interested in maritime archaeology, so many opportunities for investigating discoveries have been lost. At long last that is all changing as the Cinderella of British archaeology begins to join the rest of its family.

Summarizing the British archaeological evidence for the history of ships and seafaring in a single book has been a useful exercise. I have had to stand back from the detail of individual discoveries in order to explore overall patterns of development. Unfortunately historic sites underwater have not been managed with the same care as have the protected terrestrial monuments of Britain's heritage. This is because the underwater sites have still not been fully integrated by the Department of National Heritage into the governmental policy for the protection of sites and monuments nationally. Consequently, with no research funding and little protection of the archaeological archive, it is not surprising that the archaeological publication of maritime sites underwater has remained very limited.

Ships and boats, the vehicles or buildings of the sea, are of course central to maritime studies. Equally important, though, are the remains of ports and of the goods that were carried in ships and boats since prehistoric times. Consequently, although this book is primarily concerned with ships and boats, I have included an outline of what is known about the development of ports and have included references to goods and other things that have been transported in ships and boats. Curiously, the archaeological study of ports and their installations in Britain is a fairly neglected subject, which needs specialists to take up their cause so as to understand better their history and development.

I am particularly grateful to those who have provided me with information and those who have allowed me to reproduce their photographs and drawings. In particular thanks are due to Peter Clark of the Canterbury Archaeological Trust, Rex Cowan, Colin Martin, the Royal Commission on the Historical Monuments of England (RCHME), the Museum of London Archaeology Service, the Museum of London and the Society of Antiquaries of London. I would also like to thank Monica Kendall at Batsford, Peter Kemmis Betty and Elizabeth Nichols.

1
Maritime archaeology in Britain

Humankind's first step into an 'alien' environment was to travel by water, but that occurred so long ago that how people learnt to undertake it safely is not known, unlike the next steps into air and space. But an archaeological record of how water travel was achieved does exist, and is being discovered through the variety of sites of maritime importance that are being found in and around Britain. Off Dover hundreds of axes, swords and other items on the chalky seabed mark the probable site of a Bronze Age shipwreck of about 1100 BC; in the bed of the River Thames in central London a well-preserved Celtic-built seagoing sailing ship of the Roman period has been found with a cargo of building stone, sunk apparently in a collision about AD 150; the impression in sand of a completely decayed ship has been mapped in a Saxon burial mound of the seventh century AD on a terrace overlooking the River Deben at Sutton Hoo, Suffolk; the hull of the Tudor warship *Mary Rose*, sunk in 1545, has been raised from the muddy bed of the Solent; and a section of a Mulberry Harbour sunk off Pagham on the eve of the Normandy landings in 1944 represents a watershed event in global history.

These vivid sources of information about important events and past communities form but a handful of items from the huge archive of potential knowledge waiting to be explored by archaeologists, both amateur and professional. The seabed around Britain is known to be littered with tens of thousands of sunken ships,

the accidental losses of life and property since people first set out from the shoreline thousands of years ago. Most are probably recent, the charted wrecks having been sunk within the last 150 years (1). Many are situated in the English Channel between modern England and France in what is now one of the busiest seaways in the world, and which for thousands of years has been a prime maritime connection with the Continent. About 500 'recent' shipping losses are marked on the chart of the Dover Straits alone, but it is not known how many more older wrecks, like the Bronze Age wreck off Dover Harbour, are there. The danger of accidental loss in the Straits of Dover is ever present for the sea there forms a kind of maritime motorway, so busy nowadays that east- and westbound shipping has to be routed in lanes to avoid collision. Meanwhile, ferries ply their way across those lanes carefully avoiding both oncoming ships and the many fishing boats, yachts and motor vessels that are found closer to the shore and make this region yet more dangerous. Although accidents do occur, many of the known losses happened in the past when Britain was at war with Spain, the Netherlands, France and Germany.

The appreciation that each wreck is like a time capsule from a past age, and the need to bring submarine historic sites in British waters into the care of the nation's heritage bodies, has only recently been recognized by the British government. Although important wrecks on the

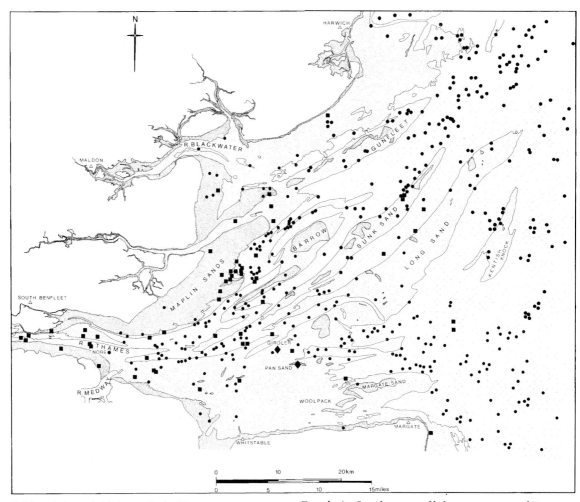

1 Map of charted ship losses in the Thames estuary.

● = reasonably intact ships probably mostly sunk after 1850; ■ = 'obstructions' that may be older wrecks; ◆ = identified early wrecks at Pudding Pan Sand (Roman) and Girdler Sand (sixteenth century). (Copyright: Museum of London)

seabed could be protected by law from 1973, the number of wrecks around the coast began to be quantified by the Royal Commission on the Historical Monuments of England only from 1992. The total recorded to 1997 is very roughly 30,000 sites, both charted and documented, from sources such as the Ministry of Defence's existing inventory of 25,000 recent wreck sites, and the assembling of other records, for example documentary references to over a thousand shipping losses that occurred in the

Goodwin Sands area off the east coast of Kent during the past 600 years. It is already clear that many of the older wrecks survived because they were buried in the blanket of seabed sand and silt, as a recent survey off East Sussex shows. In just one small area at the edge of the Channel, in Rye Bay, the Admiralty Chart shows twelve wrecks. But two local fishermen know of eleven more wrecks, as well as a further sixty 'net fastenings' – obstructions buried in the seabed that are exposed from time to time as currents move sandbanks. These are avoided when trawling as most are probably the remains of much older wrecks, like the sixteenth-century warship *Mary Rose* which was initially found in 1836 in the Solent as a net fastening. The age of some of the fastenings in Rye Bay is suggested by objects trawled up by fishermen: Roman and later pottery as well as two large medieval rudders, one dating from about AD 1200 and the other from the fifteenth century. From a later date there are the remains of the English warship *Anne*, burnt in 1690 near Winchelsea.

The care of this enormous number of underwater sites is a daunting prospect, so in 1991 the government decided to enlist the help of amateur divers by funding an archaeological training officer to be attached to the Nautical Archaeology Society, which had already established an internationally accepted training scheme. The need for this is demonstrated by the huge number of British amateur divers as indicated by the membership of the British Sub-Aqua Club which in 1994 was over 51,000 – and that represents but an unknown proportion of British divers. It is known, however, that in 1992 70,000 divers undertook 1.5 million dives in British waters.

Although ships are mainly found on the seabed many have also been found abandoned in rivers, creeks and lakes, and even on sites reclaimed as land. A few others have been found in burials on land, particularly from the Bronze Age and Saxon and Viking periods, but these have generally decayed away leaving only a slight impression in the soil. The wrecks lying in silt and sand underwater, however, have survived far better as light and air have been excluded, leaving the wood and very delicate objects in a state of waterlogged survival. The *Mary Rose* was in this condition and has told us so much about the Tudor navy: what warships looked like, how large they were and how they were built. The objects found tell a fascinating story about life on board, methods of navigation and warfare, and even about medicine.

The definition of 'maritime archaeology' is not just the history of water transport from the remains of ships, but also includes the study of ports, cargoes and debris lost on sailing routes. Moreover, it extends to the study of submerged landscapes inundated by the rising sea level following the last Ice Age. Fortunately the archaeological evidence does not always have to

stand alone, for from the thirteenth century onwards there is an increasing amount of documentary and pictorial evidence in Britain, and it is the combination of this and the archaeological evidence for an individual site that provides a very powerful tool for reconstructing the past.

The aims of maritime archaeology

To many people maritime archaeology is all about diving down to the seabed to explore ships wrecked long ago. Unfortunately this restricted view places undue stress on the diving, which is after all only a means of access to the site. In fact some of the most important ancient ship and boat finds have been discovered without diving, such as the Bronze Age boats of North Ferriby, found at the edge of the River Humber, and of Dover, found on reclaimed land. But once the initial excitement of a newly discovered ship with its historical story and the circumstances of its site is removed, we can see that the vessel was essentially a mobile building or a machine carrying people and goods between distant berthing places; and that a warship was essentially a floating castle. The ports with their quays and warehouses, and the cargoes with their packaging are equally parts of the overall picture for they sustained large land-based communities, in contrast to the small groups of people who lived on board ship. Consequently, in archaeological terms the excavation of a Roman quay in London or the discovery of Roman wine amphorae beyond the Empire in Scotland can be just as significant as finding another wreck in the seabed.

Ships

Since ships and boats are naturally central to the understanding of seafaring history, the general aim of their study must be to establish their age and place of origin, what they looked like, how they were built, how they were used, and what they show of the developments in technology. This may be difficult to discover because ship remains are often distorted, incomplete and

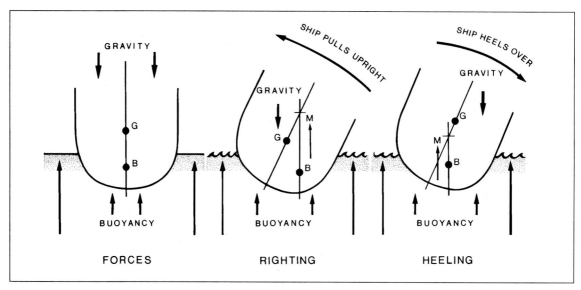

2 The forces exerted on a floating ship. (Copyright: Museum of London)

waterlogged. Nevertheless, we have sufficient experience now to know how to extract a great deal of information from the remains, particularly working from the basis that when complete a ship had limited options giving it stability, strength, and effective propulsion and steering. Nowadays, by applying computer programs for naval architecture, as if ancient vessels were modern craft, it is possible to create and examine various alternative reconstruction options quite quickly. This enables the theoretical stability, cargo loads and waterlines of reconstructed ancient ships to be established scientifically with a fair degree of accuracy, allowing quantification of the various types of goods that could have been carried as cargoes, and to establish whether or not the vessels could berth at contemporary waterfronts.

The specific objective of any ship investigation is to establish its key attributes: its original shape, weight distribution, construction, and methods of propulsion and steering. Shape and weight distribution mainly determined stability and load carrying, and the construction mainly determined its strength and how the vessel was built.

It is the stability of a ship that makes it safe. When afloat it lies at the junction of two powerful opposing forces: gravity which tries to

sink it, and buoyancy which tries to force it up out of the water. It is its balance in that state that is significant – particularly when this is disturbed by wind and waves which could cause the ship to capsize (**2**).

These forces can all be calculated by naval architects who have for a long time tested the design of ships in advance of construction, but now those calculations can be made by desk-top computer. With this in mind, then, it is possible to study such ancient vessels as the Sutton Hoo ship and discover not only what was its probable draught when afloat, but also to show that the forces to pull the ship upright if heeled were so strong that it could well have had a mast and sail.

Since there are various methods of making a ship watertight and strong, and that these varied from region to region, the study of a ship's construction is a valuable clue to the cultural tradition in which the vessel was built. Moreover, as ships and seafarers were mobile, construction ideas could spread over great distances. For example, it has been discovered recently that a late Saxon shipbuilding tradition of the tenth century in south-east England exactly matched a contemporary tradition of the southern Baltic, though the explanation for this is not wholly clear.

Many vessels, abandoned due to old age in the creeks and backwaters of rivers, or broken up and parts reused in buildings on land, normally contain little trace of the life and work of the people who worked on board. In contrast an accidental wreck preserves another dimension through the surviving possessions of the crew and remains of the cargo, and can tell us a great deal about life on board. Furthermore, for ships of post-medieval date that are documented, it is sometimes even possible to link the archaeological and documentary evidence together. But to do all this it is important to study the break-up of a wreck on the seabed by mapping and analysing the distribution of diagnostic objects, such as bronze cannons that once lay adjacent to the compass, and anchors from the bow.

Ports

Archaeologically the ports where maritime ventures began and finished are rich in information, for here voyages were planned by merchants and financed by bankers, whose homes and warehouses are valuable clues to their wealth and success. Here will be found the quays and docks, with their cranes and storage areas, and nearby the yards for building and repairing ships. The private berths will lie close to the 'public' wharfs where import duty was assessed and berthing tolls were paid (3). Some quays were for fish imports, and these came under special regulations to ensure health and safety. Out in the stream were the anchorages for the largest ships, and they were serviced by lighters that carried cargoes ashore. And throughout in the larger ports there were security arrangements, such as enclosing walls to protect the waterfront and stop the theft of goods as well as to ensure that customs duty was paid.

3 Gloucester Docks in the nineteenth century. (Reproduced by kind permission of RCHME)

Cargoes

European museums are filled with artefacts that were once part of cargoes carried by ships, but although the places of manufacture of the objects are often identified, there is a need for the publication of rather more information than is usual in archaeological reports. Particularly important are the remains of containers such as boxes, barrels and amphorae. What they carried, whether wine or nails, needs to be established together with the volume and weight of the container and its original contents. Especially interesting are cargoes of building materials, such as stone, bricks and timber, which may well have been carried down river from, say, the quarry site to a place where they could be trans-shipped to seagoing vessels.

By reconstructing the size and original weight of individual items of cargo, it is possible to equate them with the hold area of an excavated ship to see how much of any cargo could be carried at one time. Here also are clues to the former waterfront cargo handling facilities, particularly cranes. For example, in Roman Britain individual items of cargo rarely exceeded 1.25 tonnes, whereas in the Mediterranean individual items of up to 40 tonnes weight have been found in shipwreck cargoes of the same period. This implies that there were rather different arrangements in the two regions for handling heavy goods.

Sailing routes

Since a major objective is to establish the most likely route by which goods were shipped from their place of manufacture to their place of use, it is the study of the wrecks of vessels that were lost *en route* that forms a new and additionally valuable type of evidence. But there are other clues, such as the scatter of pottery and other items that fishermen trawl up from the seabed, often rubbish thrown overboard from passing ancient ships. For example, Gaulish samian ware is being trawled up in the English Channel off the Kent and Sussex coasts, and there is in the Thames estuary off Whitstable the wreck of a ship carrying a cargo of such pottery, probably to London, indicating that here was a voyage route. What is interesting is that some of these finds suggest that Roman merchantmen sailed beyond sight of the shore, and therefore may have used some form of navigation aid.

The history of maritime archaeology in Britain

Maritime archaeology in Britain is not a new subject, though it has been slow to be adopted by archaeological bodies. Its study has developed through three main stages: at first discoveries of ancient ships were noted as curios but with little description and no attempt at discovering what the vessels originally looked like; next ships were excavated and recorded, but with little attempt at interpreting and understanding them; and finally, nowadays, we are also concerned with reconstructing what vessels looked like and understanding how they were built and used. It is in this last stage that it became clear that there was a need to study ports, cargoes and even past methods of warfare. Each stage has overlapped with the next as new discoveries have inspired people to look at finds with greater interest and in more detail.

The initial 'curio' stage began with the earliest recorded discovery of an ancient ship in Europe at St Albans in the early eleventh century. Workmen building a church found, according to a contemporary account, 'close to the river bank oak timbers with nails sticking inside and smeared with naval pitch . . . They also discovered some naval tackle, namely half-rusted anchors and pine oars, a definite and obvious sign of sea water which once upon a time bore the ship to Verulamium.' Six hundred years later Samuel Pepys was intrigued by another find while a dock at Deptford Dockyard was being excavated. He recorded in his diary in 1667 that he had heard that some time earlier 'a ship of near 500 tons was there found; a ship supposed of Queen Elizabeth's time, and well wrought, with a great deal of stone shot in her, of eighteen inches [0.45m] diameter, which was shot then in use'.

By the eighteenth century the study of archaeology in Britain was in its infancy, but even then antiquaries were interested in the discovery by fishermen of Roman pots which had been trawled up in the Thames estuary off Whitstable. In 1773 an excise officer, John Pownall, decided to investigate. A fisherman took him out six miles to Pudding Pan Sand and there found a mound on the seabed 'not much larger than the hulk of a moderate-sized ship'. A drag-net was dropped to trawl along the seabed and they brought up 'a large fragment of brickwork cemented together, which I guessed might weigh about half a hundredweight [25kg], together with some small pieces of broken pans; but upon farther trial we brought three entire pans'. Roman bricks and pots have since been found over a large surrounding area suggesting that there may have been more than one wreck of the late second century AD. Several attempts have been made in recent times to locate the wreck site, but without success.

More recently there have been other ship finds, such as a clinker built vessel found in 1900 while digging out a reservoir at Walthamstow in east London. It was lying upside down on the bank of the River Lea, a tributary of the River Thames, and was believed to be covering a Viking burial. Fortunately small pieces of the boat were preserved in Walthamstow Museum, and these have recently been dated by carbon 14 to about AD 1600 and prove that there was no Viking association.

But some discoveries may have been reburied and could be re-excavated, such as a wreck possibly of medieval date found in 1833 in the Kent marshes near New Romney. A gang of workmen were deepening an old ditch called the Haven when they uncovered the vessel, 7.3m wide and 15.8m long, with a depth of 2.4m in the hold (24.5 by 51.75 by 7.75ft). It was clinker built, chiefly of oak, with some elm and fir. 'It is supposed to have been a sloop, as the

step of the mast was remaining. Many of the timbers were found firm and solid when cut with a saw; and some pieces of rope, retaining a smell of tar, were also found. Some skulls of horned animals of the goat kind, bones, it is said of men as well as animals, and some copper coins, were found on board. The situation of the vessel is full six furlongs [three-quarters of a mile] from the sea, and at the back of the Warren House.'

By 1900, therefore, the ship and boat finds in Britain had added very little, if anything, to our knowledge of the history of seafaring and trade. In fact a book on the history of sailing ships published by the Science Museum as late as 1932 referred to only two ship finds in Britain, one of Roman date discovered in London during 1910, and the other, found in 1822 in the River Rother near Rye, showing that the archaeological evidence for early seafaring was potentially important. The Rother discovery is particularly interesting as it was carefully recorded by a naval architect, and enough was published to show that it was a sixteenth-century sailing vessel lost in a storm and very quickly buried (4). The importance of the archaeology of shipwrecks was appreciated by a small group of maritime specialists, mostly members of the Society for Nautical Research, like Gerald Laird Clowes and Roger Charles Anderson, who in the 1930s examined the remains of at least one medieval wreck, their main interest being in reconstructing its place within the broad picture of the history of ships and seafaring.

Although it was only after the Second World War that the objectives of ship archaeology began to be clarified, none the less the study of two earlier ship finds had already set an excellent standard. The first was in 1910 when a Roman vessel was found on the site of County Hall, beside the River Thames opposite Westminster in central London; and the second was in 1912 not far away, downstream at Woolwich where a power station was being built. Both were recorded by staff of the London

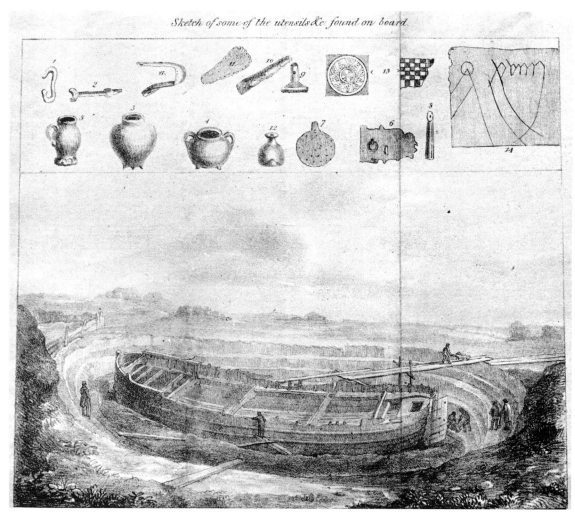

Sketch of some of the utensils &c found on board.

4 A sixteenth-century sailing ship found in the River Rother near Rye in 1822. (Reproduced by courtesy of the Society of Antiquaries of London)

County Council, and the Roman ship was even preserved and published as a booklet. The record was sufficiently detailed for the Woolwich ship to be identified in 1961 probably as the warship *Sovereign*, built by Henry VII in 1488.

In 1933 attention was drawn to the bottom of a large old ship visible at extreme low tide in the muddy bed of the River Hamble at Bursledon, near Southampton. It was examined by several maritime historians who concluded that it was probably the warship *Grace Dieu*, built by Henry V in 1418, and burnt at her moorings in 1439 (5). But nobody then attempted to use the evidence to reconstruct from the remains what this or any of the earlier discoveries looked like when complete. Indeed, it was not until 1947, when Edward Wright published a Bronze Age boat that he had found in the bed of the River Humber at North Ferriby, that a reasoned reconstruction of an ancient vessel from Britain was attempted. Even a reconstruction of the almost complete traces of the large seventh-century vessel in the Saxon royal grave at Sutton Hoo, Suffolk, which was excavated in 1939, was not published until 1963, in Sweden!

From 1958 onwards ancient vessels began to be recognized with increasing frequency in Britain, on land, in rivers and in the sea. The author found several in London, but there was then neither the time nor the facilities to undertake their full study and publication. These included a Roman barge excavated at Guy's Hospital, near London Bridge, in 1959, and a Roman sailing ship uncovered in the River Thames at Blackfriars in 1962 and 1963, but there were no agreed standards for their study. Experience gained then and subsequently by various specialists, both in Britain and abroad, established the objectives and standards that are in use today.

One of the best-recorded and published plank-built boat finds was a late Saxon vessel about a thousand years old from Graveney in north Kent. Found in 1970 during the clearance of a drainage ditch in a marsh, it was dismantled and taken to the National Maritime Museum, at Greenwich. Its eventual publication in 1978, by Valerie Fenwick, included a reconstruction and, for the first time in a British archaeological report on a plank-built boat, a naval architect's stability and performance assessment. In the same year Sean McGrail also published a national study of dugout canoes found in England and Wales, and in this he too included naval architectural assessments. But what made the Graveney boat investigation such a success was the acceptance by a museum of its timbers for recording and preservation at a time when museums tended to discard ship timbers as being too large, too wet, and requiring conservation that was too expensive (see **8**, **9**).

The need to recover all pieces of a ship for detailed cleaning, study and recording, began to be appreciated during the 1960s, particularly as a result of finds of Viking ships in Denmark and the discovery of a Roman ship at Blackfriars in London (**6**, **7**, **8**, **9**); and the historical value of ancient ships and boats as museum exhibits also became more evident. But because of their size and space requirements it also became clear that, rather than rely upon existing local museums, it was often necessary to build special ancient boat museums, as the *Mary Rose* Trust has since done at Portsmouth, and as the Nautical Museums Trust has done at Hastings.

But although the excavation, recording and study of sites imply eventual publication, it is now evident that, sadly, there is a rapidly growing backlog of archaeological publication work required for those sites on the seabed around Britain. This can only be solved when the care of British maritime sites is fully integrated into the management of archaeological sites nationally.

The archaeological problems arising from salvage law and from objects from submarine wrecks that are not normally being collected by local museums first became apparent in 1966–8 with the discovery of the wrecks of the English warship *Association*, lost off the Isles of Scilly in

5 A drawing of the fifteenth-century *Grace Dieu*, sunk in the River Hamble, near Southampton. From *The Graphic*, 27 November 1875. (Print: British Library Newspaper Library)

6 Cutting the keel of the medieval ship from Blackfriars, London (ship 3) with a chain-saw.

1707, and the Dutch East Indiaman *De Liefde*, sunk in the Shetland Islands in 1711. It was then that wreck-hunting by amateur divers became a very serious threat to historic sites, a major reason being treasure, particularly in the form of the legendary Spanish-American silver 'pieces-of-eight', and trouble quickly followed. On some sites rival groups worked simultaneously, some even setting off explosives on the seabed to break concretions whilst others were underwater. Also, as other post-medieval wrecks were found, stories circulated of the sabotage of boats belonging to rival groups, and of valuable historic objects being spirited abroad in various ways, including bronze cannons being hidden in coffins. And, of course, some divers began the long and costly path of litigation in the courts to seize exclusive rights. Many finds, such as those from the

7 Wrapping the timbers of the Blackfriars ship 3 in polythene.

8 Tracing timbers of the Saxon boat from Graveney.

Association, were auctioned off, their main record still being the auctioneers' catalogues.

There was increasing concern that the plundering of underwater sites around Britain might follow the tragic course of widespread looting that occurred to ancient wrecks in the Mediterranean. In 1964 the Council for Nautical Archaeology was established to coordinate research on British historic wrecks, and also to monitor their discovery and destruction. In due course representations were made to the government requesting that historic underwater sites be protected by law as were sites on land, and in 1973 the Protection of Wrecks Act was passed. Unfortunately it had severe limitations for it was applied by the Department of Transport only to wreck sites in the sea, but not to the fate of antiquities once brought ashore or to the fate of archaeological records, and not to

9 Traced timbers of the Graveney boat.

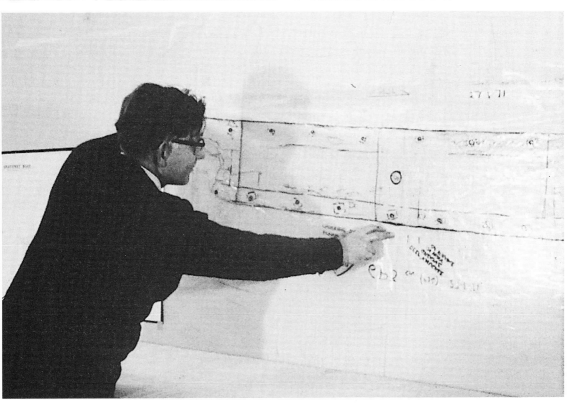

ships on land or in rivers, or to submerged land 'habitation' sites now on the seabed, and it did not release historic wrecks from salvage law.

The possibility that wrecks might be 'scheduled' under existing ancient monuments legislation was not an option, for that had already been tested some years earlier when the Department of the Environment was requested to protect the Roman barge found on land at New Guy's House, near London Bridge. After months of deliberation government lawyers finally declared that ships and boats could not be protected because originally they were chattels and not fixed structures. But had the Roman vessel been tied to a mooring post then the post and a surrounding area that included the barge could have been protected. This was ridiculous, and when the ancient monuments legislation came up for revision in the 1970s anxious representations were made to highlight this anomaly, and so it was heartening to see the 1979 Ancient Monuments and Archaeological Areas Act include provision for protecting ship remains both on land and in the sea. At last the Roman barge could be given the much needed protection. Nowadays the 1973 Act is applied to wrecks below high water, and the 1979 Act applied to sites on land.

The continuing difficulties were highlighted in 1987 when a plea, that underwater historic sites should have the same level of protection as sites on land, was made to the government in a publication entitled *Heritage at Sea*, and in its follow-up *Still at Sea*, published in 1993. These were written by a committee of specialists from various archaeological bodies and were published through the National Maritime Museum. There has been some progress since then, however, for the Department of National Heritage took over responsibility for protecting wrecks in 1992, and at the same time set up a register of maritime sites and monuments on the seabed around England. Moreover, increasing responsibility for historic wrecks has been given over to such heritage bodies as Historic Scotland and to Cadw in Wales.

One outcome of the growing public interest in nautical archaeology was the creation of the Nautical Archaeology Society in 1981, and this took responsibility for the *International Journal of Nautical Archaeology* which had been established in 1972. The Society has a growing membership of archaeologists and amateur divers, and in 1991 the government began funding through the Society the post of an archaeological training officer for amateur divers.

The methods of underwater archaeological investigation in British waters were developed in the 1960s and 1970s particularly by Colin Martin, Robert Stenuit and, of course, the *Mary Rose* team led by Margaret Rule. Pre-disturbance surveys were carried out by triangulation using tape measure, and excavation was undertaken in selected areas of sites, sometimes within a grid of scaffolding laid on the seabed. But the cold tidal seas around Britain often have poor visibility, frequently less than 2m (6.5ft), making this difficult. Nick Rule, a computer specialist, tackled this by devising the Direct Survey Method (DSM), a computer program which converts measurements from at least three fixed points around an excavation to give a three-dimensional position for any recorded spot, and which can be undertaken in very poor visibility.

The government has created an Archaeological Diving Unit that has given much help to amateur diving groups as well as providing site information to the government's advisory committee on historic shipwreck sites regarding the implementation of the Protection of Wrecks Act 1973. The Unit has done much to improve the standards of archaeological recording by amateur diving groups, though advising on the post-excavation writing up and publication of underwater sites is not part of its responsibility. Consequently, after twenty years of the administration of currently over forty protected historic wreck sites, and the licensing of their survey and excavation, most sites are still hardly published. The priority in the near future must be for the publication of this backlog of work already carried out rather than licensing yet more excavation.

In keeping with the growing study of shipwrecks there has been the archaeological study of ports. During the 1970s major excavations began on the waterfront of Roman and medieval London giving the first view of the facilities and development of a leading English port, and in time this would be compared with the results of major excavations in other important excavated medieval ports, particularly Bergen and Dublin. There are glimpses of the evidence of other ports in Britain, such as King's Lynn, Lincoln, Hartlepool and Bristol, and at last the study of medieval warehouses and merchants' houses can now begin to be put into the historical context of ports as a whole. The result is that by the 1990s the maritime economy of some Roman, medieval and later towns in Britain and abroad is beginning to take its place in urban studies, and with it has been emerging the fascinating story of seafaring since earliest times.

2
The earliest boats: the search for stability and strength

An interesting theory about how boats first developed existed some years ago: in early prehistoric times they were of logs and skin-covered baskets, but in time as woodworking tools were invented it became possible to hollow out the logs to make boats which carried people and their possessions in the dry. In due course the need to go to sea for fishing and to cross the Channel meant that vessels required higher sides. To achieve this planks were fastened to the sides of dugouts, and in time, so the theory goes, the need for the log decreased as the benefits of planks were realized, and the log became smaller until it remained only as the keel. And so plank-built boats and ships were born. However, subsequent discoveries have not supported this view as the intermediate stages have not been found among the discovered early dugouts. But the theory was a useful attempt at trying to make sense of a limited amount of data.

The shape, size and construction of very early boats must have been determined by their use and by available materials and tools. But in order to understand why and when people first took to the water in the British Isles it is necessary to reach back to the Stone Age, well over 10,000 years ago, when people were hunters and gatherers and tools were primitive. At that time Britain may have still been joined to the mainland of Europe at least in the Dover region, for the river valley that formed the Channel was still gradually being drowned by

the rising sea level caused partly by the melting of the ice caps at the end of the last Ice Age. By then Britain had a substantial population that had been living there for some hundreds of thousands of years, as is demonstrated by the many flint tools found in river gravels, such as in the Thames valley.

The earliest probable evidence for a boat in Britain belongs to the Stone Age, and is a wooden paddle of about 7000 BC found in the lakeside Mesolithic habitation site at Star Carr, Yorkshire (**10**). By then Britain was separated from the Continent, and its inhabitants were still hunters and food gatherers. It took a further 3000 years for people to start learning the skills of farming in the Neolithic period, and it seems from the extensive distribution of stone tools in the British Isles that some form of primitive 'trading' may have been undertaken, partly by water. A probable example of a dugout boat, dated by carbon 14 to about 3800 BC, was found reused in a Neolithic burial in 1989 at Old Parkbury, St Albans. Although completely decayed, its shape had survived in the ground, and in it were traces of human bones. It was about 5.52m long, 1.06m broad and 0.4m high (18 by 3.5 by 1ft), with one end rounded and the other square indicating that it was originally a boat rather than just a log coffin.

The coming of the Bronze Age to Britain, about 2200 BC, brought tools, such as axes and knives, that could be used to shape timber exactly, and so enabled planked boats to be

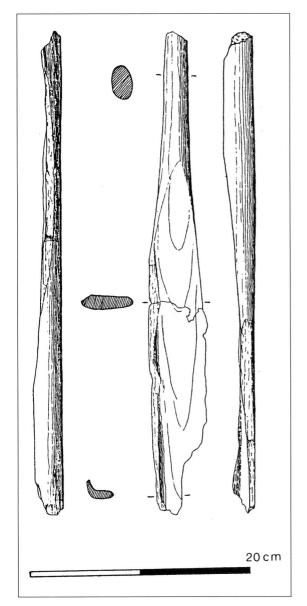

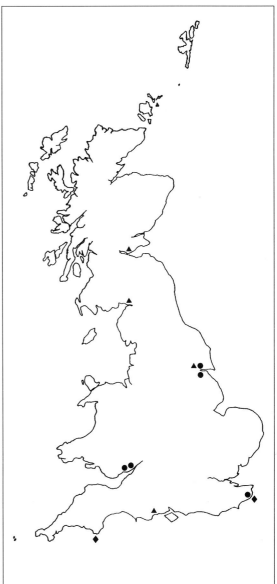

10 Star Carr paddle. From J. G. D. Clark, *Excavations at Star Carr* (Cambridge, 1954). (Reproduced by kind permission of Cambridge University Press)

11 Map of Bronze Age and Iron Age boat finds in Great Britain.

● = boat plank; ◆ = possible wreck; ▲ = other boats.

built, perhaps for the first time. For more than a thousand years Bronze Age communities developed a kind of traffic in goods, and the distribution of Bronze Age settlement sites along such rivers as the Thames reflect the importance of water transport as a means of communication (**11**). In fact a settlement at Runnymede Bridge, dating from the ninth–eighth centuries BC, had

on its waterfront a man-made sloping shore of brushwood that may have allowed boats to be beached. Shale bracelets and bronze pins were among the objects found there that had been imported from distant places, some possibly from the Continent. Another 'hard', of timber and stone rubble extending out into a river, has been found at the Bronze Age settlement at

Caldicot, Gwent; and at North Ferriby beside the River Humber were traces of a foreshore beaching site, together with part of a winch which could pull Bronze Age vessels ashore.

Itinerant metalworkers of the Bronze Age did travel between the Continent and the British Isles selling their wares, as is shown by the earliest possible shipwreck known in northern Europe. It dates from about 1100 BC and its 'cargo' was found in the 1970s scattered on the seabed of the English Channel at Langdon Bay, immediately east of Dover harbour. About 350 Bronze Age swords, daggers, axes and other items were recovered, about 50 per cent of which were of French types that were apparently not popular in Britain and are rarely found there. It seems that this was the stock of a metalworker that was being brought to Britain to be melted down for manufacture into British types of tools.

The site now lies some distance from the high chalk cliffs below Dover Castle, but about 3000 years ago the cliffs extended further out to sea and it is possible that the hoard had originally been hidden on land. But even if so, its high content of French types shows that the hoard was imported. Unfortunately the rocky seabed was unfavourable to the preservation of a wooden boat, so the exact nature of the site, either shipwreck or a hoard, will probably always remain unclear. The same possibility applies to another Bronze Age 'wreck' off Salcombe, Devon, where several swords and axes were found scattered on the seabed.

The coastline of Britain has changed during the last few thousand years, the sea level having risen around south-eastern England since the last Ice Age ended about 10,000 BC. Off Yarmouth on the Isle of Wight, for example, there are submerged peat layers of a former prehistoric land surface, in the vicinity of which fishermen have trawled up stone tools and animal bones, and in the Hastings area, particularly off Pett Level further east, the stumps of trees with fallen branches, dated by carbon 14 to about 3000 BC, are exposed at low tide.

By about 1000 BC when the Dover and Salcombe 'wrecks' had occurred, seagoing vessels were crossing the Channel, and other craft 'sailed' around the British coastline, as is suggested by the distribution of Bronze Age metal objects found on the seabed, perhaps lost from passing boats. For example axes have been found off Seaford, Bournemouth, Hull, Southend and Chesil Beach; swords have been found off Folkestone; and a copper ingot has been found off Plymouth.

So what were the vessels like? There were certainly dugout boats in Bronze Age Britain, for example Locharbriggs, Dumfriesshire, for such vessels have been dated by carbon 14 to as early as about 1800 BC but these were not seagoing craft, except in calm weather when they might have been used for fishing.

There may also have been skin-covered boats whose existence in Britain was mentioned in a lost third-century BC history by Timaeus quoted by the Roman author Pliny the Elder. Fortunately there are traces of skin boats dating from about 1700 BC at Dalgety, Fife, Scotland. They had been used as coffins in Bronze Age burials and in one were human remains and a type of pot known as a Food Vessel. The most complete boat had an elongated D-shaped plan, with a rounded bottom, and was 2m long, 0.95m wide and 0.39m high (6.5 by 3 by 1ft). Although completely decayed to a thin stain in the soil, analysis did show that it was originally made from organic materials, probably leather and wood, presumably with the former covering a basketwork of woven withies to give it shape and strength. Its shape was very much like that of recent coracles from south-west Wales, and so may have been used in the same way with the flat end facing forward. The location of the cemetery is interesting for it overlooks the north bank of the Firth of Forth opposite Edinburgh, indicating that the boat could have been used for fishing in those open waters.

But although rafts and dugouts, two different types of 'logboat', were no doubt important it is more likely that the Dover vessel which crossed the Channel had been built with skin or even planks, because such vessels could be built with higher sides and would be less prone to swamping. Plank-built vessels were particularly important since this was where the future for building large seagoing ships lay, and it is clear that Bronze Age shipwrights knew this, for they invented ways of making strong, stable, watertight hulls, and no doubt tried to develop efficient methods of propulsion and steering.

Clues to how these essential aims were achieved are found in parts of several Bronze Age plank-built boats found at North Ferriby, Brigg and Dover in eastern England and at Caldicot and Goldcliff in Gwent, though substantial parts of only three vessels, from North Ferriby, Brigg and Dover, exist to show what the vessels looked like (12, 13).

The interesting thing about all of these boats is that their planks had been sewn together edge

to edge with yew withies, and where a caulking remained to make the seams watertight between the planks (Ferriby and Dover) this was of moss held by the stitches beneath a lath of wood (14). Boatbuilders had not yet invented ribs in the modern sense to give transverse strength, but instead had fashioned raised 'cleats' of wood on the inboard faces of the planks, with holes through which thin transverse strengtheners of wood served as embryonic ribs (15).

The Dover and Ferriby boats had somewhat different shapes: the former with a broad flat bottom and the latter with a relatively rounded hull. Neither had sharp ends, but instead had a sloping plank which would have made it fairly easy to climb on board. There were no certain traces of fittings for a mast and sail or for

12 Plan of Brigg boat (top); North Ferriby boat 1 (middle); and Dover boat (bottom).

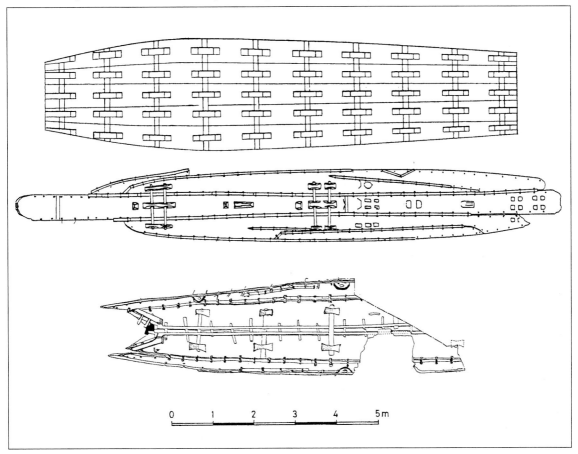

13 Reconstruction of the Dover boat. (Photograph: Canterbury Archaeological Trust)

14 Detail of stitches from Dover boat. (Photograph: Canterbury Archaeological Trust)

15 Dover boat cleat. (Photograph: Canterbury Archaeological Trust)

rowing, so it is probable that they were paddled. The construction of these vessels shows that boatbuilders had found solutions to the stresses of gravity and buoyancy by using fairly thick oak planks, and they realized that longitudinal strength was particularly important for in the Ferriby boat they made its central plank a little thicker than the side planks. In the Dover boat the two bottom planks met along the centre with two adjacent squared inboard ridges, like an internal keel. Wedges of wood driven into slots in these ridges served to hold the two halves of the boat together.

The sizes of both boats suggest that they were used for river and coastal work rather than working out in the open sea. The Dover vessel, discovered in 1992, was of oak and punt-like in shape, but only one end was excavated (**16, colour plate 1**). It was 2.2m wide, and more than 9.5m long (7 by 31ft), with a bilge plank L-shaped in section linking each side to the bottom. The sides survived to a height of about

0.4m (1ft), at which level there were stitches to attach a now missing upper plank. Although the boat was found on land, it lay in silts and sands which had been deposited in fresh water judging from the molluscs and diatoms present, and it is possible that it lay in a lagoon. This vessel may just possibly have crossed the Channel in calm weather and could have been the type of craft that was wrecked in Langdon Bay, but this interpretation depends upon the original height of its sides, the strength of its fastenings and how efficiently it was propelled.

By contrast, Ferriby boat 1 was more certainly a river and estuary craft. It was found in 1937 being eroded out of the north bank of the River Humber, at a considerable distance from the sea. Most of its bottom oak planking had survived, together with part of one side plank, and these were sewn together by withies of yew. Unlike the Dover boat it had a longitudinally curved or 'rockered' bottom to help free it from the mud when run aground. It is believed that the boat was originally about 15.9m long, 2.52m wide, with a height amidships of about 1m (52 by 8 by 3ft). It is

16 Excavation of the Dover boat. (Photograph: Canterbury Archaeological Trust)

estimated that it weighed about 4 tonnes, and could have carried a crew of twenty men. A paddle found nearby suggests how it was propelled, perhaps as a ferry across the Humber which is tidal here and 3.8km (2.3 miles) wide. Although the paddle was incomplete, a complete one has been found at Canewdon, near Burnham-on-Crouch, Essex, and is dated by carbon 14 to about 950 BC. It was 2.07m (6.75ft) long, and had a knob on its shank allowing it to be held comfortably.

Although there are many uncertainties about the reconstructions of the Dover and Ferriby vessels, particularly concerning the height of their sides, at least their basic shapes are clear. However, this does not apply to the substantial remains of another Bronze Age boat, a vessel found in 1888 at Brigg, beside the River Ancholme, a tributary of the Humber not far from South Ferriby (**17**). The boat was re-excavated in 1973–4 and was dated by carbon 14 to about 860–820 BC. Parts of six oak

planks, sewn together with split strands of poplar or willow, formed a flat structure about 12.2m long and up to 2.7m wide (40 by 9ft). The seams between the planks were made watertight with a caulking of moss under laths of split hazel. In the centre of each plank were the usual raised 'cleats' each with a hole through the middle, and in these were thin transverse oak timbers up to 3cm (1in) thick and 13–17cm (5–7in) wide which linked the planks together. There are two opinions on the original shape of this vessel. On the one hand the remains may have been the flat bottom of a box-like vessel with vertical sides, and on the other hand the vessel may have had a rounded hull in cross section.

It is fascinating to see in these vessels the search by boatbuilders for a stable design and a strong watertight hull. What is also interesting is that by 1000 BC these objectives were achieved without nails or substantial ribs, both of which apparently had yet to be invented. The method of fastening planks together by sewing was perhaps derived from having sewn leather sheets together in skin boats, though the planked vessels were all 'shell-built', their skin of planks having been fastened together before their embryonic 'skeleton' of transverse timbers was positioned. Moreover, at that time there is no evidence for propulsion by sailing or rowing, only paddling, so any effort to cross the Channel must have been considerable. The discovery of several Bronze Age vessels with a similar sewn and cleat construction, in south Wales and eastern England, indicates that this was the general technique of boatbuilding at that time.

The use of wooden nails, trenails, to fasten timbers together was a great advance on sewing for they were much stronger. However, the earliest evidence for the use of trenails in boatbuilding in north-west Europe is found in

the Hasholme dugout canoe, discovered in 1984, but even here their use was limited (**18**, **19**). Lying close to the modern River Humber, and only 9km (5.5 miles) from North Ferriby, it has been dated to about 300 BC. The boat is of oak and was about 12.78m long, with a maximum beam of 1.4m, and a height of 1.25m (42 by 4.5 by 4ft). Its bow was closed by timbers that were locked into place by transverse beams fastened through cleats to give a flat sloping stem. At the stern there was a vertical board that slotted into the log to give a squared-off end and a seat held by trenails.

The notion that a boat is somehow imbued with life dates back at least to *c*. 300 BC, for on either side of the bow of the Hasholme boat was an eye or 'oculus' to allow the vessel to 'see' while on a voyage, as in many modern boats. There was no mast to carry a sail or oar pivots

17 Brigg boat.

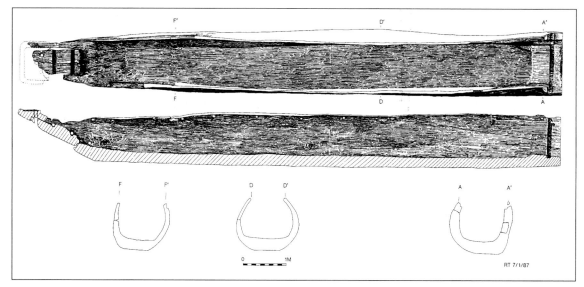

18 The Hasholme dugout canoe. (Copyright: National Maritime Museum)

19 The Hasholme boat excavation, North Humberside 1984. (Photograph: Martin Millett, University of Durham)

for rowing, so it was presumably paddled, there being room for nine pairs of paddlers who must have been standing since the sides were too high for kneeling.

Although the Hasholme boat was found in a modern field, the ancient waterway in which the vessel had sunk having long ago silted up, the excavators did uncover surprising evidence that it was wrecked. Its 'cargo' of food, represented by over 200 pieces of bone, mostly cattle but with some of sheep or goat, horse and red deer, indicated that it was well stocked with joints of prime meat.

Several other dugouts have been found dating from about the same period as the Hasholme boat, from Shapwick, Poole and Holme Pierrepont, indicating the widespread use of these craft on inland waters, presumably for hunting, fishing, fowling, reed gathering and even as ferries.

No pre-Roman plank-built boats of the Iron Age have yet been found in Britain, so there is a gap of about a thousand years extending to about AD 150 before the date of the next discovery of a plank-built vessel. That next find is fundamentally different in construction for it was a seagoing sailing ship with massive ribs and broad planks which were fastened together with numerous iron nails. Great advances in shipbuilding technology had therefore occurred in the intervening centuries, and how they occurred is possibly partly suggested by a vessel found at Hjortspring on the island of Als, Denmark. It dates from about 300 BC and was about 18m (59ft) long, with lime planks which had been sewn together. But in its case the 'ribs' of hazel sticks lay not through the cleats but instead on top of them, and were lashed to the cleats. Perhaps here is an intermediate stage in the development of the framing of a boat that was to reach its peak by the first century AD, at least in central and north-west Europe, for the size of frames were no longer constrained by the size of the holes in the cleats.

Meanwhile, far away in the Mediterranean other types of ships, including some that had planks sewn together, were exploring the edges of the known world. It was claimed that a Greek adventurer, Pytheas, was the first to sail through the Pillars of Hercules, the modern Straits of Gibraltar, to explore the northern seas in the third century BC. He seems to have landed in south-western England where he was told that tin, mined nearby, was taken by hide boat probably for sale on the Isle of Wight, six days' sail up the Channel. Other Mediterranean seafarers evidently followed whose voyages are unrecorded except for archaeological remains. One of these lay only 30m (98ft) from the rugged cliffs of the Lleyn Peninsula, near Anglesey, where amateur divers found the lead stock of a classical Mediterranean anchor of the second century BC. It was decorated with a symbol of Venus, and although only 1.18m (3.75ft) long and weighing 71.5kg (157lb), it may have been lost during attempts to save a small Greek trading ship from loss. Furthermore, a hoard of Greek silver coins of about 120–60 BC has been found at Penzance indicating another seafaring contact, perhaps while trading in tin. It was only a matter of time before yet another Mediterranean adventurer, Julius Caesar, would decide to explore the northern regions and try to conquer them.

3
Late Iron Age and Roman ships

When Julius Caesar waged the earliest known sea battle in northern Europe in 56 BC he was fascinated by the ships of his enemy, the Veneti, a native Celtic tribe of north-west Gaul. He made it clear in his account of the battle that by then shipwrights in northern Europe had discovered how to build fairly large strong ships, with massive ribs, iron nail fastenings, sails and side rudders, and he described how the vessels were ideally suited to the harsh seas and tidal shores. But how and when such important developments in ship technology had occurred in the previous centuries will not be known until plank-built ships of the Iron Age are found.

The Romans won the sea battle, but not without much difficulty for Caesar had been unable to capture the fortified headland settlements of the Veneti before they escaped in their ships to other strongholds. A major reason was that his own ships, built in the completely different Mediterranean tradition, were unsuited to the rough northern tidal shores. An answer seemed to be for him to ram the enemy vessels, but he soon found that their hulls were too thick. The actual solution was to cut their shrouds, the ropes that held the mast, and so remove their only form of propulsion. 'After that', Caesar explained, 'it was a soldier's battle in which the Romans easily proved superior.'

He described the Veneti ships as being built solidly of oak, with exceptionally high bows and sterns, and with much flatter bottoms than the Roman ships. They had ribs a foot (c. 30cm) wide, which were fastened with iron bolts as thick as a man's thumb. Their anchors had iron chains, their sails were made of raw hides or thin leather, and between the planks was a caulking probably of moss. Pliny the Elder, writing a little over a century later, mentioned that much further east, near the modern Netherlands, the Belgae used a caulking of reeds in their ships.

Although there are no contemporary representations of the Veneti ships, a native coin of the first century BC exists of the neighbouring continental Atrebates, and shows a vessel with a projecting 'forefoot' at the base of the bow. There are also two coins of the Belgae in south-east England which show a sailing ship with a forefoot, a side rudder to starboard, and a mast that evidently carried a square sail (20), but whether or not these, the earliest known representations of seagoing sailing ships in northern Europe, were typical of Celtic vessels is not known.

The Veneti anchors were perhaps like a late Iron Age iron anchor dating from the earlier part of the first century AD that was found in 1881 in a hillfort at Bulbury, in Dorset. Although only 1.44m (4.75ft) long, it too possessed an iron chain 6.5m (21ft) long and probably had a removable stock. Its size was only suited to a smallish craft, as might have used the Sherford River that flows past the fort on its way to Poole Harbour 3km away (2 miles).

20 Bronze coin of Cunobelin showing ship, from Canterbury, AD 20–43. (Copyright: Museum of London)

A more detailed contemporary impression of a Celtic vessel is a delightful gold model of a sailing boat found in 1895 in a hoard of the late first century BC, at Broighter on the east bank of Lough Foyle, in Ireland. It is also one of the earliest known certain representations of a sailing vessel in northern Europe, and has a mast and yard for a square sail, as well as nine oars a side for rowers who sat on thwarts. At the stern is a side rudder, fastened through a hole in the gunwale, and on the other side is another hole indicating that there was probably originally a pair. Unfortunately, it is not clear if it represents a skin or planked boat.

The scarcity of Veneti coins in Britain suggests that they were shippers rather than merchants carrying exports from the Continent before the Roman conquest. British exports included gold, metals, grain, cattle, hides, slaves and hunting-dogs, and in return the Mediterranean imports that reached Britain included wine, figs, glass and pottery. Their route to Britain across the west end of the Channel is traced by the distribution of Dressel 1A amphorae of the first century BC which contained Italian wine. Sherds of these also indicate the location of some of the earliest known seaports in north-western Europe: at

Mount Batten in Plymouth, Hengistbury Head, Christchurch Harbour, and Poole Harbour, and in France they have been found at Bordeaux on the Gironde and at Alet near Saint-Malo. Dressel 1A amphora sherds and later Roman pottery found on the seabed off Yarmouth, Isle of Wight, also suggest an anchorage for ships sheltering from gales.

The berthing arrangements at these ports are indicated by excavations on the contemporary shoreline at Hengistbury, where a shelving gravelled 'hard' would allow waggons to be driven down beside a beached ship at low tide for loading and unloading.

After the Roman invasion of Britain in AD 43 there was an influx of Roman merchants whose trade was carried via the Rhône, but once in the Celtic regions of central and northern Gaul, the goods were apparently barged down the Rhine, Seine and Loire to the coasts of Germany and Gaul in native Celtic vessels. Other goods were carried across the neck of land between south-western Gaul and Spain via the Garonne.

Just how the native Romano-Celtic seagoing sailing ships were built now seems clear from the wrecks of merchant vessels found in the River Thames at Blackfriars, London, and at St Peter Port, Guernsey, in the Channel Islands (**21, 22**). They had the constructional characteristics that Julius Caesar described for the Veneti vessels, and were completely different from the Roman ships in the Mediterranean for they were largely 'skeleton-built', with planks nailed to a pre-erected skeleton of substantial ribs.

Blackfriars ship 1, found in 1962, had sunk probably about AD 150 near the waterfront of Roman London while carrying a cargo of building stone quarried near modern Maidstone, on the River Medway, Kent (**23–27**and **colour plate 2**). The cargo had shifted to one side suggesting that there had been a collision. The vessel was sharp at both ends with the planking nailed to the stempost and sternpost. Its beam was about 6.12m (20ft), and, judging from the curve of the stem and sternposts, the original

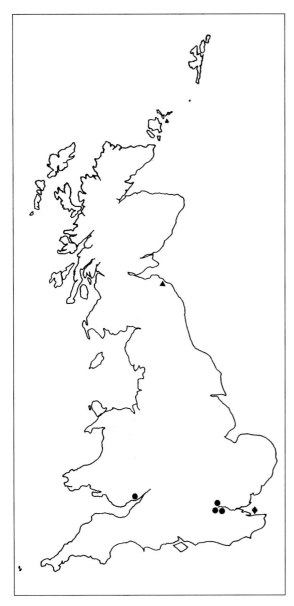

21 Map of Roman boat finds in Great Britain.
● = ships and boats; ◆ = wreck; ▲ = rudder.

mast height relative to diameter it seems that the mast was originally about 12.7m (41.5ft) high. There was no evidence of the method of steering, though the remains of a similar vessel found in 1899 at Bruges, Belgium, and now dated by carbon 14 to the second or third century AD, included a massive side rudder that was probably originally strapped to the hull.

Instead of having a true keel, Blackfriars ship 1 had two thick and broad central planks which gave the vessel a strong flat bottom. To these were nailed a series of massive bottom ribs each cut from a tree-trunk. Then lower planks about 50mm (2in) thick were nailed to the ribs, each nail having been driven through a pre-drilled hole from outboard, with the point bent over and hammered down onto the top of the rib (see **25**). The outermost plank attached to the bottom on each side was also the lowest plank of the side, and to this were nailed the side ribs and planks. The shipwright was evidently concerned about leakage, for between the planks he had used a caulking of hazelwood shavings and pine resin, apparently applied to the edge of each plank before the next was fastened into place. Also, the hollow cone-shaped iron nail heads were filled with a caulking of thin strips of hazelwood set in pine resin to stop leakage into the nail holes in the hull.

Although the last voyage of Blackfriars ship 1 was evidently down the River Medway and up the Thames to London, this was probably an unusual voyage since the hull planking was infested with the borings of the mature *Teredo* 'shipworm' and, to a lesser extent, *Limnoria*, both of which only live in the sea. As these borings existed up to at least 1.22m (4ft) above the bottom they show that the usual waterline was a little above this. A computer analysis shows that this waterline lay just below the point of maximum stability, and that the ship could normally carry a load of about 50 tonnes. An earlier voyage route at sea is suggested by an unfinished millstone, possibly from the Namur region beside the River Meuse in Belgium, found lying in the bow.

length of the vessel was about 18.5m (60ft). The surviving sides, which, when restored from their collapsed state, gave the height up to 2.16m (7ft), show that there must have been a deck. In the centre of the vessel was a hold about 5.7m (18.75ft) long lined with planks, and at its forward end was the rectangular socket or step for a mast, 0.25m (10in) wide, which was cut into a rib. By using various traditional 'rules' of

The other Romano-Celtic seagoing sailing ship had been wrecked in the harbour of St Peter Port, Guernsey, shortly after AD 285, judging from the evidence of coins. It was a similar vessel with a mast also stepped into a rib, and was found in 1982. Only the bottom remained (see 22), but this was covered inboard with a thick deposit of tar, the remains of a cargo, showing that the ship had been burnt before sinking. It had a triple planked 'keel' and this and its planks and ribs were of oak. It too had the same cone-headed nail fastenings as had Blackfriars ship 1, though these were caulked with moss. Between the planks was a caulking of wood shavings, either of oak or willow.

The hold of the St Peter Port vessel was not lined with planks, though at the stern there were the collapsed traces of a deck cabin, with roof tiles, parts of a hearth, and even cooking utensils for three people. The ship was about the same size as the Blackfriars ship for its keel was 13.9m (45.5ft) long compared with 11.3m (37ft) in the Blackfriars ship, but its maximum width at the ends of the bottom ribs was 3.9m (12.75ft) whereas the Blackfriars ship was 4.7m (15.5ft) wide.

Reconstructing the rig of these two ships is difficult for had they been like those depicted on the Belgic coins from Colchester and Canterbury (see 20), both minted by King Cunobelin, the sails would have been square, the simplest form then probably known in northern Europe. But the ideal position for the mast and its single square sail is slightly forward of amidships, so the fact that in these discovered vessels the masts were well forward of that, at about one-third of the vessel's length from the bow, suggests that a fore-and-aft sail would have

22 Plans of Blackfriars ship 1, London (top) and the St Peter Port ship, Guernsey.

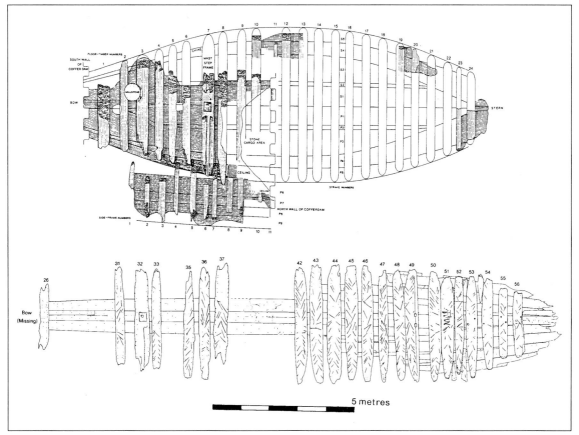

5 metres

23 Mast-step area of Blackfriars ship 1. (Photograph: Museum of London Archaeology Service. Copyright MoL)

worked better and allowed the ships to sail closer to the wind. However, such sails are not known to have existed in northern Europe until over 1000 years later. One of the major problems in the study of the merchant shipping of Roman Britain is that there are no known local representations, a strange absence which suggests that ships did not feature highly in the life and traditions of the British except as mere transports of goods and people.

The cargoes that such seagoing ships carried are found in the earliest Roman occupation deposits in British ports like London and Colchester dating from the century following the invasion of AD 43. They include pottery, glass, grain, marble, wine and olive oil that had been imported from the Mediterranean region, especially southern Gaul, Spain, Italy and even Greece, and it seems that these goods mainly reached Britain by being shipped up the Rhône

24 Votive coin in mast-step of Blackfriars ship 1. (Photograph: Museum of London Archaeology Service. Copyright MoL)

and then down the rivers Seine, Loire and Rhine, as well as down the Garonne to the Atlantic, before being carried to Britain. As there is almost no indication that ships rounded Spain from the Mediterranean, this would explain why most of the Roman vessels that have been found in central and northern Europe are of the Celtic tradition of shipbuilding, and why none was built in the Mediterranean. When reconstructing seafaring and ports in Roman Britain, therefore, it seems that it would be wrong to imagine that the merchant ships were of Mediterranean type. This is not to say that some features were not borrowed from the Mediterranean seafarers, in particular the placing of a coin under the mast for luck, as was found in the step of the Blackfriars ship in London (see 24). In that

instance a bronze coin of the emperor Domitian lay reverse uppermost with the figure of Fortuna, goddess of luck, touching the base of the mast.

The cross-Channel routes to Britain are described by Strabo in the first century AD, who said that ships sailing from the Rhine followed the coast to the port of Boulogne, and then across to Britain. In this way seafarers kept in sight of land. But whether or not this was general is not certain, for some Roman pottery has been trawled up from the bed of the Channel, like a Roman amphora found 32km (20 miles) south-west of Newhaven, indicating that voyages did occur out of sight of land.

There were, of course, the usual shipping hazards which are known from archaeological evidence and classical documentary sources: collision, fire, piracy, winter storms and poor navigation. The fourth-century author Libanius even seems to refer to the fate of ships stranded at low tide on the Goodwin Sands, where 'the

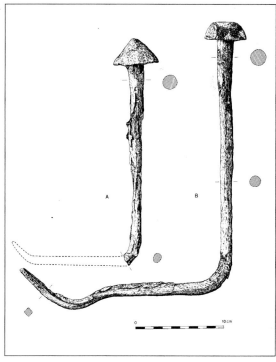

25 Hooked nails from Blackfriars ship 1. (Copyright: Museum of London)

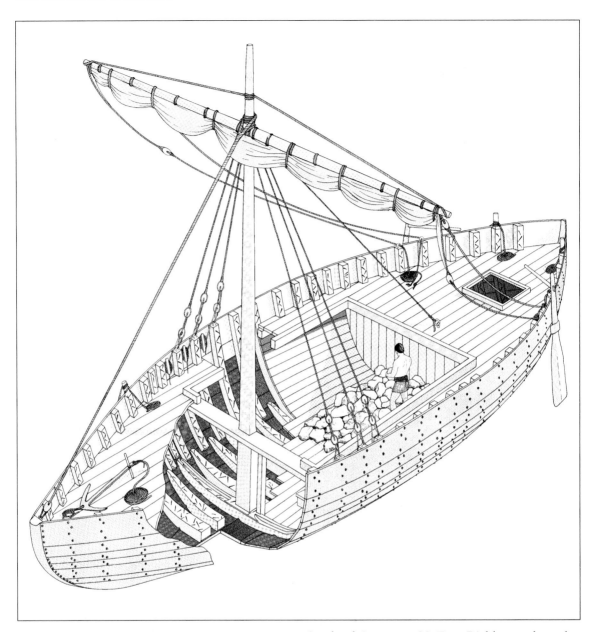

26 Cut-away reconstruction of Blackfriars ship 1.
   (Copyright: Museum of London)

vessel sinks by degrees, the sand yielding to its weight'. The discovery of Roman pottery in the Goodwin Sands lends weight to this reference and suggests that substantial parts of Roman ships could be found there in the future. These merchantmen were probably of Celtic type, for their characteristic cone-headed iron nails have been found at the legionary fort at Inchtuthil,

Scotland, in use AD 83–7, at Richborough, and in third-century deposits in London, suggesting a widespread distribution of those ships. The first-century nail is particularly important since it is only a century later than Julius Caesar's reference to the ships of the Veneti.

The locations of wrecks are valuable clues to the cause of their loss, and although the sites of

27 Suggested stages of collapse of Blackfriars ship 1.
   (Copyright: Museum of London)

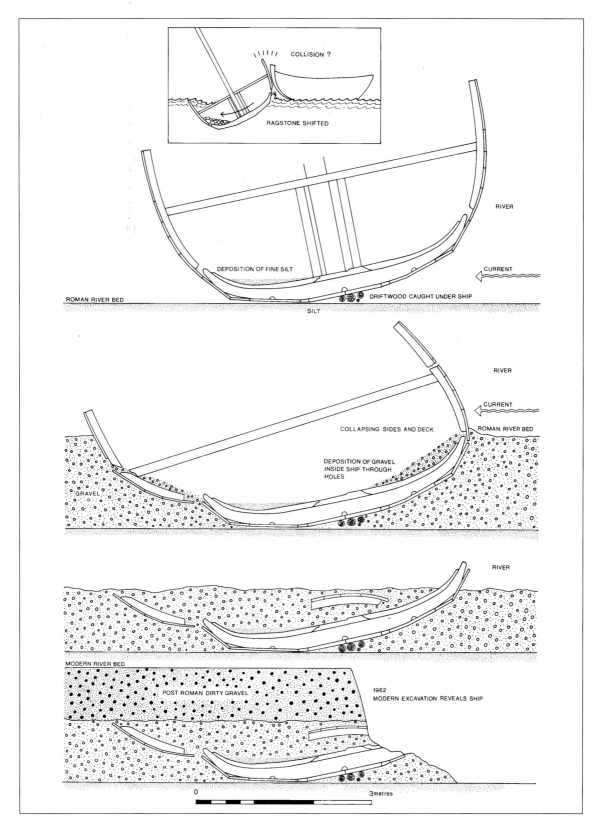

COLLISION ?

RAGSTONE SHIFTED

RIVER

CURRENT

DEPOSITION OF FINE SILT

ROMAN RIVER BED

SILT

DRIFTWOOD CAUGHT UNDER SHIP

RIVER

CURRENT

COLLAPSING SIDES AND DECK

ROMAN RIVER BED

DEPOSITION OF GRAVEL
INSIDE SHIP THROUGH
HOLES

GRAVEL

RIVER

MODERN RIVER BED

POST ROMAN DIRTY GRAVEL

1962
MODERN EXCAVATION REVEALS SHIP

0   3 metres

several Roman wrecks are suspected, some may simply be debris from anchorages. Six pottery mortaria stamped CAVARIUS have been recovered from the Ooze Deep in the Thames estuary; nineteen Roman and one Greek coin of the late third century AD have been found off the Needles, Isle of Wight; a group of amphorae of the late first to second century AD has been recorded outside St Peter Port, Guernsey; and a large number of pots, mainly of Gaulish samian ware, have been trawled up from Pudding Pan Sand off Whitstable, north Kent. Naturally there was the inevitable loss of life by shipwreck, one poignant record being on a tombstone from Chester. It refers to the death of a soldier 'who was awaiting promotion to centurion'. The inscription was intended to conclude in Latin 'he is buried here', but the last word was not inscribed presumably because his body was never recovered.

Of the great variety of goods that were imported into Roman Britain, little is known about how most were packaged while in transit. Wine, olives and fish-sauce were carried in pottery amphorae, and wine was also carried in wooden barrels, but no clear trace of either boxes or sacks has been noted. Whenever such containers are found it is most important that their weight and volume are calculated, for only then can they be related to the capacity and displacement of actual ships. Since barrels are often found reused as well-linings on land, their original volume and filled weight can easily be assessed. They were among the heaviest individual items that are known to have been shipped to Roman Britain, none being greater than about 1.25 tonnes. This contrasts with individual items of cargo found in Mediterranean wrecks of Roman ships which go up to about 40 tonnes (a block of marble). The difference may well reflect the limitations on berthing and loading facilities imposed by the tides in northern Europe. Consequently, northern ships were apparently small compared with the largest Mediterranean merchantmen, and this would account for the small storage

rooms in a late first-century warehouse found in London, as compared with the rooms in warehouses found in the Mediterranean area. The London building was 6m (19.75ft) wide and about 50m (164ft) long, with rooms only about 4.3m (14ft) wide opening onto the quayside.

The organization of trade between Britain and the Continent is referred to in a remarkable group of inscribed altars with dedications to the goddess Nehalennia, which were set up at shrines near Domburg and Colijnsplaat in the Netherlands. They show that the East Scheldt was an important staging place for trade, and, together with inscriptions from Cologne, Castell by Mainz, Bordeaux and York, show that trade was in the hands of merchants (*negotiatores*), and that the shipping was carried out by *nautae* and corporate groups of shippers (*societates*), often involving shipping agents (*actores navium*). The mechanics of Roman port administration are not too clear, but in major ports like London there was probably an official who collected the tax (*portoria*) levied on imports. This would be part of the tax which each town and its surroundings would pay through the *procurator* who is known to have been based in London. An inscription dedicated to the *procurator* by an imperial slave responsible for collecting such tolls has been found in Spain.

The only extensive study of the waterfront of a Roman port in Britain is in London, but how representative its timber quays were of other ports in northern Europe will not be clear until other sites have been excavated. One of London's earliest traders was Aulus Alfidius Olussa, born in Athens, who was buried in London probably in the 70s or 80s AD, so he knew the waterfront that the excavations have revealed. Initially, soon after the city was founded about AD 50 ships were apparently either moored in the river for offloading into lighters, or were beached on a falling tide, for near modern London Bridge there has been found a sloping gravelled 'hard' that would enable wheeled vehicles to pull alongside beached ships at low water. From the 70s onwards to about AD 250 London's berthing facilities were improved with timber quays and jetties (28). A study of the microscopic diatoms in the river silts shows that the river was brackish, and therefore tidal, and a very careful comparison of levels has shown that in front of the quays initially there was probably only about 0.5m (1.5ft) of water, but that later Roman quays were built into deeper water (29). Jetties were necessary for the berthing of larger ships, but not for shallow draught vessels, like oysterboats, which could tie up at the quays. Part of a jetty has been found, but, curiously, no mooring posts have been definitely located. Concentrations of Gaulish samian ware, amphorae and masses of oyster shells beside the quays presumably reflect dumped cargo

breakages and other rubbish, suggesting that the waterfront was zoned for specific shippers or cargo types.

Apart from the cross-Channel traders there were also coastal vessels carrying goods from one British port to another, such as pottery from the Dorset region, and building stone needed in regions where there was no suitable stone. The Blackfriars ship 1 was sunk in London about AD 150 while carrying Kentish ragstone from the Maidstone region on the River Medway, and this cargo could have been used in any of the fine houses or public buildings in that city. The voyage of about 112km (70 miles) must have relied heavily on the tides, and the total

28 Reconstruction of London's early Roman quays. (Photograph: Museum of London Archaeology Service. Copyright MoL)

29 Late first-century timber quay found in Pudding Lane, London. (Photograph: Museum of London Archaeology Service. Copyright MoL)

quantities of stone carried by many ships were enormous. For the city wall alone, built soon after AD 200, it is estimated that about 45,000 tonnes of the stone had to be transported to the city. Also, there was a considerable use of Lincolnshire limestone for architectural mouldings and inscribed carvings in London during the third century AD. Quarried near Stamford and Corby the individual blocks weighed up to three-quarters of a tonne each and were presumably lifted into the holds of ships by cranes. They were probably barged down the rivers Welland and Nene and shipped around East Anglia to the Thames. The movement of such heavy and bulky cargoes would have caused much wear and tear on ships, and repair facilities were necessary once in port. But hardly anything is known about such ancillary services to Roman shipping in Britain, though in London a wooden writing tablet has been found which refers to the building of a ship and to the making of the tiller for a rudder.

The many navigable rivers of Britain were highways for heavy bulk goods, and these were no doubt carried in flat-bottomed barges. Their importance is illustrated by a recent study of Roman villas in Kent, Surrey and Sussex which shows that four-fifths were sited within 5km (3 miles) of a river. But little is known about how goods were transported up and down rivers, though the barges themselves must have been extremely shallow draught vessels, like the vessel which was found in a creek close to a Roman timber quayside near Guy's Hospital, by London Bridge. It was abandoned about AD

180, and is estimated to have been at least 16m (52ft) long (of which 6.7m/22ft was found), about 4.25m (14ft) wide, and approximately 1m (3ft) deep amidships. It could carry about 6 tonnes of cargo at a draught of about 0.4m (1.4ft), and was of native Celtic build, similar to the Blackfriars ship 1, though fastened together with hooked iron nails with flat heads. It is not clear how this vessel was propelled, but it is noticeable that no forked iron tips from 'set poles', traditionally used for punting, have yet been found in Roman London. In contrast they are shown on the Iron Age boat model from Broighter, Ireland, and are common in the Roman Rhineland region. Towing *may* have been used in some river craft as is suggested by the forward position of the step for a mast or towing post in a flat-bottomed Romano-Celtic vessel found at Barlands Farm, Magor, near Newport, Gwent (30). This vessel was originally about 11.3m (37ft) long, 3.2m (10.5ft) wide and possibly less than 1m (3ft) high.

Fishing provided an important source of food, and the bones of many fish have been found in London. Cod, bass, carp and eel could have been caught by hook and line, sprat were more likely to have been caught by net from a boat in the estuary, and Black Sea Bream was probably fished in the Channel where it is caught today. Many of these, including oysters, were presumably kept alive in water-filled tanks or barrels carried in the boats during their journey back to port. The distribution of seafood, especially oysters which are found on almost every Roman site in Britain, is one of the least studied aspects of Roman Britain in spite of being a very important part of the diet. Some of the fishing in rivers may well have been from dugout boats, such as a third-century vessel from Wisley on the River Wey, Surrey, which

30 Romano-Celtic boat found at Barlands Farm, Magor, near Newport, Gwent. (Photograph: Glamorgan Gwent Archaeological Trust)

was 3.66m (12ft) long and is now preserved in Weybridge Museum.

The Roman navy

During the second and early third centuries AD the Roman navy was divided into a number of fleets that were scattered around the Empire. One of these, the *Classis Britannica*, the 'British Fleet', was based around the Channel crossing between the ports at Boulogne and Dover and provided the main official link between the Continent and Britain (**31**). Shipping was expected to make the crossing by night and by day, judging from the presence of substantial lighthouses – one at Boulogne and two at Dover (**colour plate 3**). There is no reason to believe that a fleet of that name existed during the first or in the later third and fourth centuries, and it is inappropriate to ascribe all references to naval activities in Britain during those periods to the fleet of that name.

During the first century Roman warships were an inseparable part of the invasion force in Britain, for they carried soldiers and supplies, provided a means of speedy communication, and explored the coast ahead of military actions on land. No military or naval ships or boats of

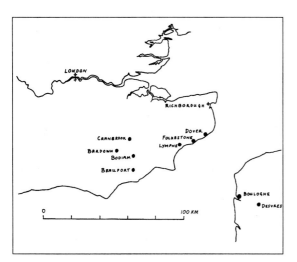

31 *Classis Britannica* sites. Major sites shown by ● and minor sites by + . Ports existed at Boulogne, Dover and Lympne, and a villa at Folkestone. Ironworking sites lay in the Bodiam region.

this period have yet been found in Britain, though a side rudder, only 1.65m (5.5ft) long, was discovered in the first-century fort at Newstead and was from a vessel only about 1.4m (4.5ft) high. This was probably one of the smaller military craft in use in Britain, perhaps like those that have been found at military bases on the Rhine and Danube.

The use of warships as a wing of the army of conquest was different from their subsequent use. The building of Hadrian's Wall in the 120s delineated the northern boundary of the Empire and it is about that time that the *Classis Britannica* enters history, with units of its men actually helping to build the wall. At about the same time a naval fort of the *Classis Britannica* began to be built at Dover but was not completed. After a pause, construction began again on the same site about AD 130–40, and the fort continued in use until the beginning of the third century.

There is some uncertainty about the nature and function of the *Classis Britannica*, particularly at its permanent bases, indicated by tiles stamped CL BR (**32**), at Dover, Lympne and Boulogne where sea ports provided a secure Channel crossing. In the naval fort at Dover were barrack blocks perhaps housing 600–700 men, possibly enough to crew five warships; and there were granaries, all within a rectangular defensive wall with gates near the middle of each side, encircled by a V-shaped ditch. Outside the fort was a timber waterfront, but no sign of how it was used. Stamped tiles also occur in a Roman villa at Folkestone, between Dover and Lympne, where perhaps a senior naval commander lived overlooking the Channel.

There are also concentrations of stamped tiles at the Wealden ironworking sites on the border of East Sussex and Kent at Bardown, Bodiam, Cranbrook and Hastings. It may seem puzzling that the navy should be involved in ironworking, especially as it probably had no excessive need for iron. But as the ironworking sites were evidently in imperial ownership, the

32 *Classis Britannica* tile stamps from (top) Cranbrook, Kent, and (bottom) Folkestone villa.

both on land and at sea. Some of these may have been based on new coastal forts, particularly the Saxon Shore Forts between East Anglia and Portsmouth, one of which was at Dover and was constructed over the remains of the *Classis Britannica* fort.

We can glimpse how the new naval arrangement operated through the misguided efforts of Marcus Aurelius Mausaeus Carausius, commander of the Roman fleet based at Boulogne who had been given responsibility for tackling the German pirates raiding merchant shipping in the seas off Britain and northern Gaul. Although he had intercepted many of the barbarian ships he was, in AD 286–7, found not to be restoring all of the seized booty to its owners. Maximian, the Roman emperor, ordered his execution, whereupon Carausius assumed the title of emperor and took control of Britain. The coins of Carausius often depict warships. His reign was short since he was assassinated in AD 293 by his finance minister Allectus, but three years later the new emperor in the west, Constantius Chlorus, reinvaded Britain and restored it to the Roman Empire.

Probably dating from immediately after these events was the construction of a Roman ship found in London on the County Hall site opposite Westminster (33, 34). This vessel was unusual in northern Europe for although the tree-ring study shows that it was built locally, it was constructed of oak according to the Mediterranean shipbuilding tradition, almost certainly by a shipwright from that region. It was originally carvel built, the edge-to-edge planking being held by mortice-and-tenon joints, and was 5.06m wide, 2m high amidships and at least 19m long (16.5 by 6.5 by 62.4ft). Although only part of the hull near amidships had survived enough remained to show that it had a deck supported on stanchions (35). It was 'shell-built', the planking having been constructed before the ribs were inserted, unlike the 'skeleton-built' Celtic ships. The tree-ring dating and the study of coins found under some ribs show that it was built about AD 300, and was

solution may simply be that as the iron was extremely heavy it was much more efficient to transport it by water, and what better way than in government ships. All the CL BR ironworking sites lie close to rivers, so once the iron had been barged to the sea it could then be shipped by military transport vessels to anywhere on the coast and on navigable rivers in the provinces of Britain and northern Gaul. In this way the *Classis Britannica* had a similar use to that of the *Classis Germanica* on the Rhine which was involved in the quarrying and distribution of building stone.

The Roman army throughout the Empire was reorganized during the third century, and the named fleets were apparently disbanded. In Britain the centrally organized legions on land were replaced probably by irregular units of lightly armed infantry and cavalry, and a series of naval squadrons were probably set up to tackle the increasing barbarian raids and piracy,

33 The County Hall Roman ship, London, as excavated in 1910. It shows the ribs and longitudinal keelson on the ship's bottom, and the collapsed side. (Copyright: Corporation of London)

34 The County Hall ship being removed from the site on its timber platform. This was to be placed on wheels and pulled through the streets of London to the new London Museum. (Copyright: Corporation of London)

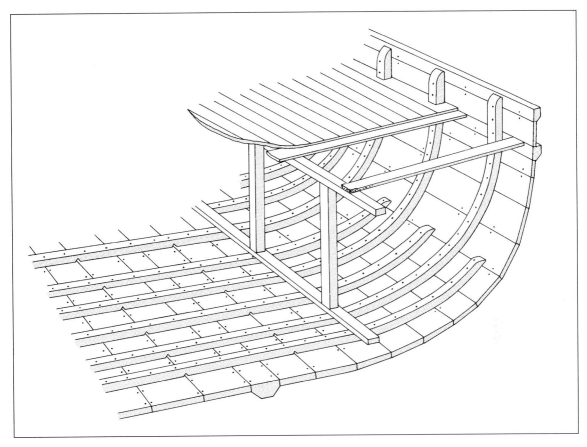

35 Perspective of County Hall ship. (Copyright: Museum of London)

abandoned by the river bank soon after. Very few other examples of Mediterranean-type vessels have been found in central and northern Europe, but those that have been discovered were locally built and were associated with Roman military forts. They were therefore presumably government vessels built according to regulations laid down in Rome, and this may well explain the significance of the County Hall ship, which could have been built for an official purpose just after the re-establishment of Roman rule in Britain by Constantius Chlorus in AD 296. It is unlikely that it was a merchant ship, particularly as London's quayside was then in a state of decay and was separated from the city by a riverside defensive wall.

Little is known about specific Roman naval and mercantile activity in Britain during the fourth and early fifth centuries, though the importation of goods from abroad had become very limited compared with earlier times. A little Mediterranean pottery did find its way into south-west England during the fifth century, but only for a short while and it is not clear if it was shipped around Spain or along the rivers of Gaul. The Roman economy and barbarian raids had so affected Roman Britain that ports like London had declined, until the Roman age passed away. But out of the chaos of the collapsed Empire was to be forged Saxon England, as new Germanic settlers joined the native Celts. And with them came an entirely different maritime tradition.

4
The invaders

From the fourth to the eleventh century AD there were three major waves of settlers into Celtic Britain – firstly the Angles, Saxons and Jutes who came from modern northern Germany and Denmark during the fourth to the sixth century; secondly the Vikings from Denmark and Norway who settled mainly from the ninth to the eleventh century; and finally the Normans from northern France who invaded England in 1066. It is not surprising then that their collective culture soon swamped that of the Celtic Britons many of whom were in turn perhaps driven further west, to Cornwall, Wales, Ireland and Scotland. This is, of course, a great over-simplification of the situation, for there was no doubt also a merging of the Celtic and invading peoples to make the hybrid culture that is the English.

With these people came an entirely different maritime tradition from those of the Celts and Romans. They had long open vessels whose hulls were clinker built with overlapping planks. But this has left a major question of what happened after the fourth century AD to the shipbuilding tradition of Celtic carvel planked ships. Did it remain in the Celtic areas of western Britain for some centuries, or did it die out entirely? Any future boat finds dating from the fifth century and later in those regions will be particularly interesting.

By the sixth and seventh centuries the southern half of England was occupied by a number of Saxon kingdoms which in the eighth century became dominated by the kingdom of Mercia, and in the ninth century by Wessex. During this period seaborne trade slowly developed (36), initially under the Frisians, a coastal people living in the northern Netherlands round to southern Denmark. From the seventh century we begin to see the slow growth of new towns and ports in northern Europe, one of the best known being Dorestad on the Rhine, where excavators have found houses for merchants built along the river bank as if the beach was the market place, and with it were coins, weights and balances for the merchants, cooking utensils for feeding crews, and even tools to repair ships.

Until a large seventh-century Saxon ship was discovered in 1939 in a royal grave at Sutton Hoo, Suffolk, nobody had any idea that these peoples had such complex and sophisticated shipbuilding techniques at that early date (37). This great open clinker built vessel was 27m (89ft) long with a beam of about 4.5m (14.75ft), and a height amidships of about 1.5m (5ft). It was banana-shaped with pointed ends rising to about 4m (13ft). It had a plank-like keel 0.87m (3ft) wide and only 0.4m (1.4ft) thick, and nine strakes a side, each made from a number of planks joined end to end with scarfs. The whole plank structure was held together by iron rivets, and inboard the vessel was strengthened by twenty-six ribs held to the planks by trenails. As the ship had been reused in a royal burial, possibly of King Raedwald

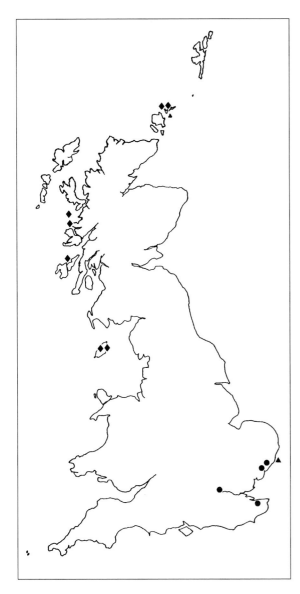

36 Map of Saxon and Viking boat finds in Great Britain.
●= Saxon boats; ◆= Viking boat burials; ▲= rudder.

'thole pins' for fastening oars showing that it was originally propelled by at least ten pairs of rowers. These lay fore and aft of the middle of the vessel, but none was found amidships as if the centre was used for another purpose. Was the midships area for a kind of throne and the ship a royal 'barge', or was it a large cargo ship? We may never know, though it is clear that the ship had been used on the water for some time since a few of its planks had been repaired.

Under an adjoining burial mound were traces of a smaller early seventh-century clinker built boat. One end was sharp and the other apparently missing, but originally it was about 6.85m (22.5ft) long, 1.8m (6ft) wide and 0.9m (3ft) high. However, these were not the earliest clinker built craft found in Britain, for in 1862 a smaller vessel was uncovered at Snape, 15km (9 miles) north-east of Sutton Hoo, in a grave of a man of high status dating from the latter half of the sixth century. It too was completely decayed, though the stain in the sand with rows of characteristic iron rivets showed that it was about 14m (46ft) long and 3m (10ft) wide, and had eight or nine strakes each side. But not all Saxon vessels were plank built for nearby were two other graves, excavated in 1987–8, with decayed dugout boats, one of which could carry a man and was about 3m (10ft) long, 0.52m (1.75ft) wide, 0.35m (1ft) high, and was sharp at both ends rather like a fast modern canoe.

The ancestry of Saxon ships is believed to be fairly well known in southern Scandinavia, beginning with the Hjortspring boat, carbon 14 dated to about 370 BC from the island of Als, Denmark. This was a paddled vessel, 19m long, 2m wide and 0.7m deep amidships (62 by 6.5 by 2.4ft), with planks sewn together and tied to the ribs. The next stage, represented by the Nydam boat found in a bog in south Jutland in 1863, is tree-ring dated to about AD 310–20. It was originally about 23.7m long, 3.75m wide, and 1.2m high (77.75 by 12.4 by 4ft), and was clinker built with iron rivets holding the plank overlaps, but its nineteen ribs were lashed to cleats on the inboard faces of the planks.

who died in AD 624–5, most of its internal fittings had been stripped out and it was not possible to tell if originally it had a mast and sail. In the centuries that followed the burial the hull decayed away leaving only a grey stain in the sand, with the rows of rusted iron rivets outlining the edges of the planks and keel.

However, by burying the entire vessel the Saxons had ensured that traces of its gunwale would survive, and on it were the impressions of

37 The Sutton Hoo ship being excavated in 1966.

In these long open vessels, whose shell of planks was constructed before the skeleton of ribs was inserted, we see the change from paddling to rowing, and from sewing to the use of much stronger iron fastenings holding the planks together. But as yet there is no evidence of propulsion by sail in clinker built vessels of the fourth and fifth centuries. So did the Angles, Saxons and Jutes row across the North Sea or the Channel in vessels of Nydam type? Opinions are divided and we must await further discoveries.

In fact it is not really clear when sails were first used in Scandinavian shipping. Various possibilities have been suggested and evidence given, such as pictures of ships with masts and sometimes square sails that are found on stone carvings from the Swedish island of Gotland in the Baltic, and on a strap end in the French National Museum. These are thought to date from as early as the seventh century, but iconography is so difficult to date. Even the great ship at Sutton Hoo may have had a mast and sail, as a computer analysis of its hull shape and weight distribution shows that it originally had a very strong righting force when heeled, as if the vessel was designed to counteract the heeling force of a sail. But no trace of fittings for a mast and sail was found.

There are further problems in our understanding of that period for although the Saxons were the latest settlers in eastern England, the main traders in the seventh and eighth centuries were apparently Frisians from the coastal area of the Low Countries. Nobody knows what their ships were like, though some specialists have suggested that they had developed a type of vessel called a Hulc, though as this type was first documented about AD 1000 in London it is difficult to see how it can be traced back confidently to the eighth century.

What is not in doubt, however, is that ports were developing in England during the seventh and eighth centuries, at London (Lundenwic),

Ipswich (Gipeswic), York (Eoforwicceaster) and Southampton (Hamwih), for example. Of these, Hamwih is the most extensively excavated, though not its waterfront along the River Itchen. It had a regular layout of gravelled streets running parallel to and at right-angles to the river bank, with timber buildings facing the streets, and areas behind for latrines, wells and rubbish pits. Those pits contained evidence of the port's extensive trade: from Germany there is fine glassware, various types of pottery (Badorf, Tating and Pingsdorf types), and Niedermendig lava millstones, and from France there was pottery probably from the Beauvais region beside the Loire. At Ipswich the site of the port has been identified on the north bank of the River Orwell, and here again imports of glass and German pottery testify to cross-Channel trade.

In London the middle Saxon port has been found 1.6km (about 1 mile) west of the walled Roman city, in an area now known as Aldwych ('the old town'). In the seventh century this was known as Lundenwic, and by the 720s Bede described it as 'a mart of many peoples coming by land and sea'. It was then a port for the Mercian kings, and it is not surprising that it lay on a sailing route to three of the great continental trading towns of this period, Quentovic, Dorestad and Domburg.

Although there has been little investigation of the waterfront of Lundenwic, pottery has been found there which had been imported from northern France during the late seventh and eighth centuries, and from the Rhineland in the ninth century, and also there were considerable quantities of pottery from Ipswich beside the Thames estuary. Fishing was quite important, though marine species were represented by less than 17 per cent of fish bones identified, but included herring, plaice, flounder, conger eel, cod, whiting, hake, gurnard, red sea bream and brill.

By the tenth and eleventh centuries the archaeological and documentary evidence for ships, trade, cargoes and ports in Britain is more extensive. Excavations in London have shown that the Viking raids of the ninth and tenth centuries had caused the citizens to abandon the Middle Saxon settlement site at Aldwych and build a new town within the Roman city wall. On the waterfront of the defended city the king established three 'common quays' or public berthing places for trading ships, at Ethelredeshythe (later renamed Queenhithe), St Botolph's Wharf and Billingsgate where duty on imported goods was collected. It is believed that there were beach markets there, and also at two other berthing sites, Dowgate and Vintry, which were used by German and French merchants.

Excavations have shown that in the Billingsgate area and at Dowgate the waterfront then had broad artificial beach embankments about a metre (3.25ft) thick, of timbers, stones and clay, probably for ships to run ashore, thus facilitating the loading and unloading of cargoes (38, 39). At Billingsgate there was also a timber revetted inlet or tidal dock 5m (16.5ft) wide

with sides about 2m (6ft) high, and with two mooring posts at its entrance. Further west were the timber supports of a jetty for larger ships.

A mass of discarded red-painted pottery of the twelfth century, believed to be cargo breakages imported from the Rhineland, was found with the embankment at Dowgate, showing that German merchants were present some time before the earliest record of their 'guildhall' nearby which would later become the London headquarters of the Hanseatic League.

These finds of imported goods link with Ethelred's fourth law code of about 1000 which states that in London goods were being imported from Normandy, northern France, Flanders and Germany. This includes the earliest record of berthing tolls in Britain and applies to Billingsgate where one half-penny was paid for a small ship, and one penny for a larger ship with sails. A 'keel' (*ceol*) and a 'hulc' (*hulcus*) paid fourpence each, and a ship with a cargo of planks paid one plank; and on Sunday, Tuesday and Thursday only was a toll payable for cloth.

The next earliest English port regulation is also for London, and is the 'law of the Lorraine

38 A reconstruction of the tenth-century waterfront excavated at New Fresh Wharf, London. (Copyright: Museum of London)

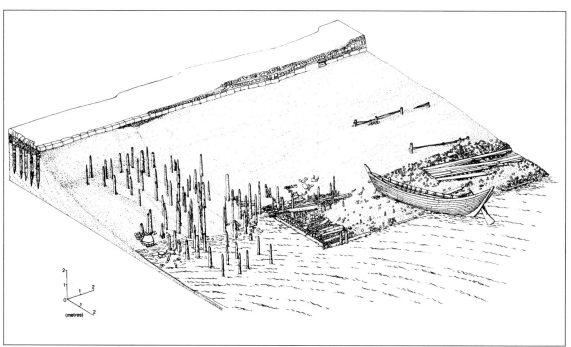

39 Late Saxon waterfront beach of timbers, stones and clay, City of London, typical of the tenth and eleventh centuries.

merchants', of about 1130. It shows that these merchants mainly imported barrels of wine, though other goods ranged from cloth to silver and gold tableware from as far afield as Constantinople. These were carried in ships via the rivers Danube and Rhine, and then across the narrow seas to the Thames and London. On arrival each ship had to raise its ensign, presumably to identify itself, and the crew would sing 'Kyrie eleison'. Then the cargo of wine could be sampled by opening just one barrel at the cost of one penny a stoop. The ship would then sail on to reach a hithe or landing place, presumably Dowgate, and there would wait two ebbs and one flood tide when no trade was allowed except with the king. This gave the king's chamberlain and sheriff the first chance to buy part of the cargo, but it had to be paid for within two weeks. Afterwards the Lorrainer could sell to others, first to merchants of London, then to those of Oxford, then of Winchester, and finally to anyone else. The

Lorrainer who sold his goods onboard needed only to pay the wine custom to the king, but if he sold it ashore then further duty was due. These regulations show just how tightly the king controlled his income from trade in English ports, and how international was London's merchant population at that time. It also shows how the archaeological remains enable the written record to be pictured.

But what were such ships as the Hulc and Keel like? There are many late Saxon and Norman illustrations of ships and boats, the best known being on the Bayeux Tapestry showing the Norman invasion of England in 1066. They illustrate open clinker built vessels sharp at both ends, some propelled by oars and others by a square sail on a mast situated amidships. Steering was by a side rudder fastened to the starboard side near the stern. Sadly, it is not possible to link these to the named types, although this has been attempted.

The only substantial part of a Saxon boat so far found in England was excavated in 1970 in Graveney marsh near Whitstable in north Kent, and has been dated by carbon 14 to the tenth century (**40, 41, colour plate 4**). The bottom of the vessel and the stern had survived and indicate a boat originally about 13.6m long, 4m broad, 1m high amidships and 2m high at the ends (44 by 13 by 3.2 by 6.5ft). It was of oak and had a thick plank-like keel to which its planks were attached and to each other throughout by iron rivets. The overlapping planks were caulked with wool treated with vegetable tar, and the ribs were fastened to the planks by trenails of willow. It is not clear how it was propelled, though as reconstructed it had a hull shape and weight distribution that gave it such stability that it is possible that it carried a sail. Also it could carry a cargo of about six tonnes, though as the low sides amidships would have caused the vessel to be swamped rather easily in rough seas it is most likely that the boat was a coastal rather than a cross-Channel craft. There were clues to former cargoes lying in the bottom of the boat: fragments of roughly shaped lava querns originally from the Rhineland but were perhaps being distributed from a major English port like London, and abundant traces of hops, presumably for brewing beer. Although the hops could have been grown locally it is equally possible that they were imported from France where at that time hops were grown in monasteries.

That there were larger seagoing ships is shown by the discovery of two side rudders of the eleventh century, trawled up from the North Sea off Southwold, Suffolk, which are 3.91m and 4.36m long (13ft and 14.3ft), and were from vessels whose sides were roughly 2m and 3m high near the stern (6.5ft and 10ft).

Viking ships of the ninth and tenth centuries were also clinker built, their size and

40 Graveney boat as found.

construction being given by several boat burials found on the islands of Man, Skye, Arran, Orkney and Colonsay, and on the Scottish mainland at Oban, and near Inverness. In each case the boats had decayed away leaving only a scatter of iron rivets. On the Isle of Man, for example, the boat found at Knock-y-Doonee remained as about 300 iron rivets, and indicated a vessel about 9m long and 2.5m wide (29 by 8ft). Traces of another boat burial were found

41 The Graveney boat. Provisional plan based on drawing by the author.

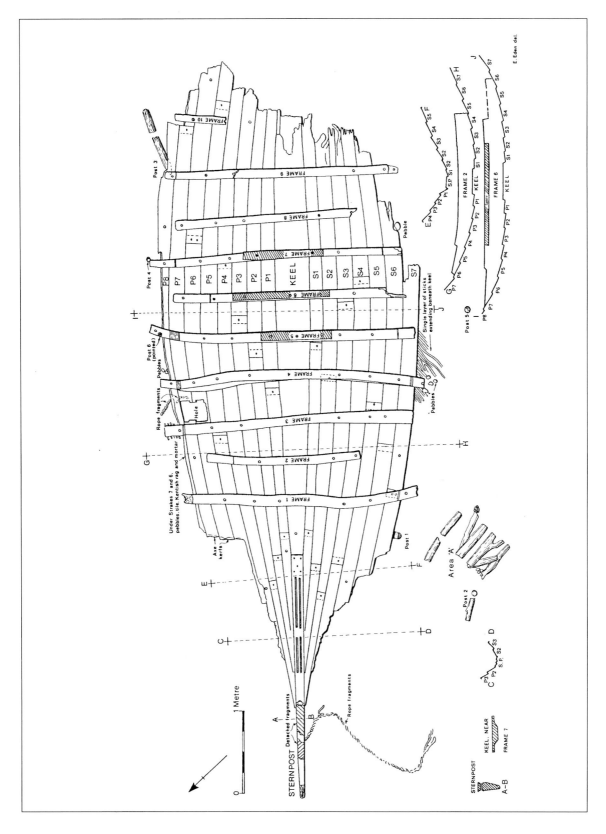

in 1991 at Scar on the island of Sanday in the Orkneys, and here too about 300 rivets marked the lines of at least five strakes per side. The boat was about 6.5m long and roughly 1.5m wide (21 by 5ft) and in it were the bodies of a man, a woman and a child. These Viking vessels were quite small compared with seagoing Viking ships like the eleventh-century vessels recovered from Roskilde Fjord in Denmark which were between 12m and 28m (39ft and 92ft) long, so the British boats were probably used locally for fishing and ferrying rather than for long sea voyages.

The Anglo-Saxon Chronicle mentions the presence of larger ships in Britain carrying the Viking raiders who attacked many Saxon settlements, and it was probably from one of these that a fascinating hoard of equipment, lost about AD 1000, has been recovered from the River Thames at London Bridge. It comprised seven iron battle axes, a woodsman's axe, six spearheads, a pair of tongs and a grappling hook.

Many boat fragments found in the waterfronts of late Saxon and Norman London are especially interesting for they show some variety in local shipbuilding during the tenth and eleventh centuries. Although all were from clinker built vessels, some had planks fastened together with iron rivets in the typical Viking fashion; but others had plank fastenings of small pegs of willow or poplar, and the plank of yet another was fastened to a keel with hooked nails. Most had a caulking of hair, though moss was used instead between the pegged planks. This variety of fastenings has been found elsewhere in southern England in late Saxon boat fragments. For example at Medmerry, Selsey, a plank possibly of about AD 800 was apparently pegged, though a tenth-century boat fragment from Newport, Gwent, had iron rivets and hair caulking. The Graveney boat was a little different for some rivets had been driven through pegs, and was like the construction of part of an eleventh-century vessel found in 1990 at Buss Creek, Southwold, Suffolk.

This variety of construction is not found in the Viking areas of Scandinavia and was evidently a characteristic of late Anglo-Saxon England during the ninth to the eleventh century. What is interesting is that the pegged planking with moss caulking is identical to that found in the Slavic area of the southern Baltic coastline of Poland and north-eastern Germany, and the hooked nail fastenings are probably a feature of shipbuilding in the Low Countries area where the Frisians had settled. It is as if Anglo-Saxon shipbuilding in southern Britain reflected the cosmopolitan origins of its settlers and traders (**42**). In fact one piece of planking from London had a moss caulking held in place by a batten and iron staples and had a tree-ring pattern for north Germany, whereas another London plank, grown in the south-east England region, had Viking shipbuilding characteristics similar to those found in the ships from Skuldelev, Denmark, and had presumably been built by a Viking shipwright in England. A puzzle, however, is how the Slavic method of shipbuilding had been introduced into England. Perhaps it dates back to the sixth century when Saxon settlers arrived from north Germany where both pegged and riveted planking are thought to have existed.

During the whole of the Saxon period, from the fifth to the eleventh century, there were also boats of skin, in Ireland at least, and in England there were dugout boats, a number of which have been dated by carbon 14. A particularly interesting group of nine vessels from the River Mersey dating from about the eleventh century show similar characteristics, with rounded ends and a small projection. Another dugout, found in 1987 at Clapton, near Hackney in east London, by the bank of the River Lea, is of oak and is tree-ring dated to AD 950–1000. It was 3.73m long, 0.65m wide and 0.4m high (12 by 2 by 1.3ft), and had rounded ends with a

42 Types of clinker plank fastenings in Europe, seventh to thirteenth century AD. (Copyright: Museum of London)

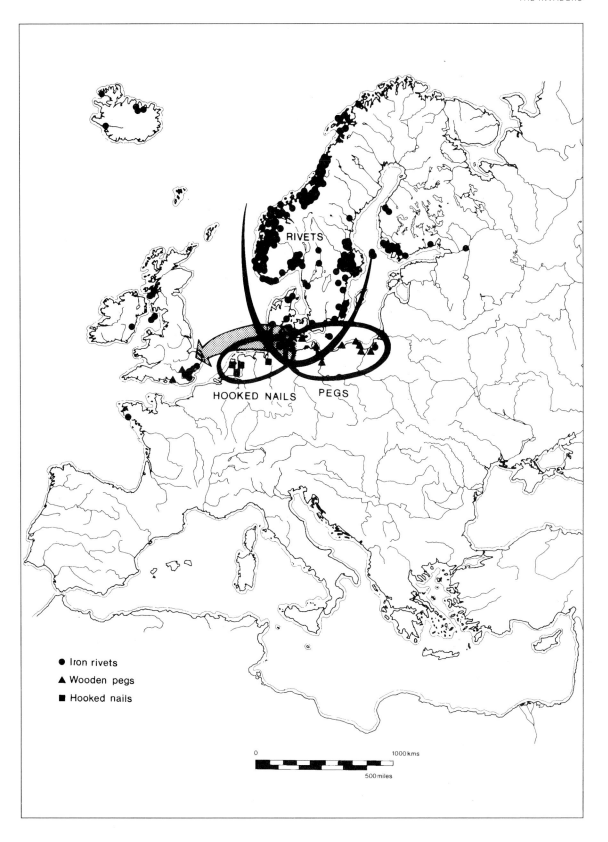

RIVETS

HOOKED NAILS

PEGS

● Iron rivets
▲ Wooden pegs
■ Hooked nails

0   1000 kms

500 miles

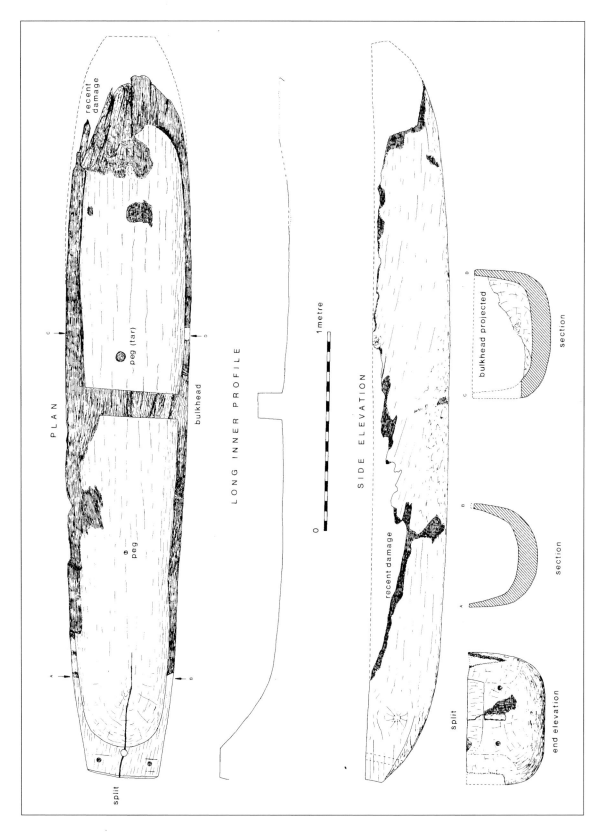

PLAN

peg (tar)

peg

recent damage

bulkhead

split

LONG INNER PROFILE

SIDE ELEVATION

recent damage

split

0

1 metre

bulkhead projected

section

section

end elevation

43 Drawings of the Saxon dugout boat from Clapton, near Hackney, London.

bulkhead across the middle for a seat (**43**). Of special interest were clear toolmarks of adzes and an axe showing how the boat was fashioned from the log (**44**). A hydrodynamic study, made by Sean McGrail, found that at a draught of 26cm (10in) it would carry a load of 120kg (264lb), enough, say, for one man (70kg) and 50kg of 'cargo'. Of further interest was the building by Damian Goodburn of a full-sized working reconstruction which showed that the boat would have been quite difficult to manoeuvre by paddle but was much easier by punting with a pole.

What is not known is whether or not all this variety of construction also reflects a variety of ship and boat forms, or were all vessels similar to the long open Viking ships? Perhaps there was some variety for, as we enter the eleventh century, this would partly account for the development of various ship types in Britain during the succeeding centuries.

44 Toolmarks in the boat from Clapton, near Hackney.

5
Medieval seafarers: 1200–1500

The period from 1200 to 1500 saw some of the most important developments in the design, construction, steering and propulsion of ships since the invention of plank-built vessels in northern Europe over 2000 years earlier. Ships became much larger, went from a single mast and sail to three and four masts with several sails, and changed from side to sternpost rudder (**45**). Therefore by about 1400 the technology existed for the handling of the large ships that equipped the seafarers of Europe to launch the Age of Exploration later that century. Moreover, ports had developed from little more than beaches to having quays and even docks. All these developments were partly brought about by the period of greater stability and economic growth which followed the Norman invasion of England in 1066, and, although wars and feuds continued in Europe, there was generally an increasing need for bigger, stronger and safer vessels to carry larger and more valuable loads on greater non-stop voyages than before. Mediterranean ships began to sail the Atlantic route around Spain and Portugal, and across the Bay of Biscay with goods for northern Europe, so no longer were the rivers of Europe the only important routes of transportation. But the links with the Mediterranean had already been forged by the Normans who in the eleventh century captured Sicily and southern Italy, and by the Crusaders who from 1096 sought to establish Christian rule in the Holy Land. But these extended sea voyages brought great dangers, not only from storms and difficult coasts but also from pirates. One of the best known was the renegade Flemish cleric Eustace the Monk who plundered French and English shipping until he was captured in the Straits of Dover and executed in 1217.

The growing size of medieval ships

The remains of ships are particularly valuable clues to the size of medieval ships in English waters since documentary records are frankly confusing and not very reliable. For example a vessel called the *White Ship* is said to have carried 300 passengers when it was wrecked in 1120, but this may be an exaggeration. In 1214 merchant vessels that could carry up to fifteen horses were impressed into the king's use, and at Shoreham in 1229 some Italian merchants were only allowed to charter ships which could carry less than sixteen horses, since larger vessels were required by the king. By the end of the thirteenth century the size of ships began to be indicated by their capacity in tuns, though it is far from clear how this was calculated. For example when Edward I crossed to Flanders in 1297 some ships from Yarmouth ranged from 120 to 240 tuns. At the same time the port regulations of London record that wine ships were arriving with cargoes of up to 200 tuns, and that ships with larger cargoes had to moor in the River Thames instead of at quays. By 1375, when the Spanish attacked and destroyed a fleet of English merchant ships off Brittany,

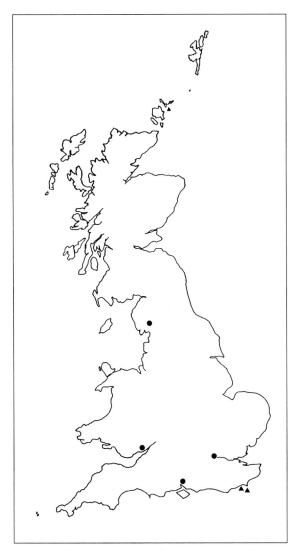

45 Map of medieval boat finds in Great Britain.
●= boats; ▲= rudders.

the larger vessels are recorded as ranging from 200 to 300 tuns. So the general pattern was for merchant ships to get larger.

A consequence of this increased maritime activity was the development of major medieval ports from the eleventh and twelfth centuries onwards, such as Southampton, King's Lynn, Newcastle upon Tyne, Hartlepool, York, London and Poole. But although they are frequently very well documented, particularly after the twelfth century, it is only archaeology that enables them to be pictured, though up till now there has been little extensive excavation of their waterfronts. However, some excavations are giving clues to medieval river levels. This is important because most ports lay beside rivers where shipping access was controlled by the ebb and flow of the tides. Hence, although the association of tide times and heights to the phases of the moon has long been recognized, the earliest known tide table in the world comes from the thirteenth century. This relates the time of high tide at London Bridge to the age of the moon, and helped merchants to predict the arrival of their ships.

There were at least three major types of large northern European seagoing merchant ship that were carried on the tides to the ports during the medieval period: long open vessels of the Scandinavian ship tradition, possibly including the Ceol or Keel; banana-shaped Hulcs; and Cogs with their angular ends (46). There were other seagoing types too, such as the Buss and the Barge, as well as Mediterranean vessels such as the Galley, and of course many smaller local river and coastal craft such as Farecosts and Shouts, but to what extent these were variations of the three major types is not clear. The problem is trying to identify what they looked like, and here some of the illustrations of ships on medieval port seals in Europe are helpful.

Scandinavian ship tradition

The long clinker built ships which followed the Viking and Saxon 'tradition' are shown on the Bayeux Tapestry, and the remains of vessels of this type have been found at Skuldelev, near Roskilde, in Denmark dating from about 1000. One of those has the tree-ring pattern of the Dublin region so it was evidently built there; and it is in Dublin that parts of other ships of this type have also been found, helping to confirm that the port was founded by the Vikings in the ninth century. The Dublin ship fragments show that up to the mid-twelfth century the vessels were just like the Viking ships of Scandinavia in their shape, construction and method of propulsion; but that after the Anglo-Norman

46 Three medieval ship types from northern European port seals: (left) Scandinavia; (centre) Hulc; (right) Cog.

invasion of Ireland in 1169 their planking became thicker, plank scarfs longer, fastenings bigger, ribs heavier and masts thicker. The ship fragments had mostly been reused in waterfronts, and substantial parts of three thirteenth-century vessels enabled minimum estimates of their original lengths to be calculated at between 16m and 18m (52ft and 59ft).

English ships of Scandinavian type were also common in south-east England during the twelfth and thirteenth centuries for they are shown on town seals, such as those of Romney, Winchelsea (**47**), Hythe (Kent), Pevensey, Folkestone, Faversham, Sandwich, Dover, Portsmouth and Yarmouth (Norfolk), and on the seal of St Bartholomew's Hospital, London. These had a large side rudder or steerboard with a tiller at the top usually on the right-hand side facing forward near the stern, this apparently giving rise to the term 'starboard'. Also, each had a square sail set on a mast amidships, which was a great improvement on the forward mast position of the Celtic ships for it enabled the vessels to sail closer to the wind. Sail handling was particularly important, and in a new development the seal of Yarmouth not only shows a bowline, a rope attached to the side of the sail to enable it to be pulled round to catch the wind better, but also a bowsprit which enabled the bowline to pull the sail even further round.

The most visible improvement to the safety and comfort of the crew featured on some thirteenth-century seals is a small castle at each end, the forerunners of the permanent 'forecastle' and sterncastle of ships today. They acted as watch towers, as a cover for the helmsman and, if needed, as fighting platforms.

47 Seal of Winchelsea.

As the hull structure became more substantial, so it was necessary for the deck to be supported strongly. The projecting ends of deck beams are shown on seals as lumps on the sides of ships, though actual beam ends have been found in some medieval ships in Sweden and Germany, and in the fifteenth-century wreck of the *Grace Dieu* near Southampton (**48** and see **5**). Of interest is a fourteenth-century timber quay at Trig Lane in London which had similar projecting beam-ends suggesting that the carpenter was a shipwright.

As only small fragments of broken-up medieval ships and boats were frequently reused in waterfronts at ports, it is difficult to know if they came from ships or boats. Nevertheless, a study of the many pieces of thirteenth-century vessels found in Dublin shows that planks up to 21mm (1in) thick were from 'boats', and planks over 30mm (1.5in) thick were from 'ships', whatever those terms may mean. The planks were mostly of oak, and were clinker built with iron rivets holding the overlaps together, and in the joint was a caulking of hair to make it watertight. They were all 'shell-built', the shell of planks having been constructed before the ribs were added.

Similar boat fragments have been found at Magor Pill on the Welsh side of the Severn estuary, dating from about 1250, and in London. In one case, from the Custom House site near the Tower of London, there is sufficient structure to allow an estimate of the minimum size of the entire vessel to be conjectured (**49**). It had a flat bottom, sharp ends, and was clinker built, the vessel originally being at least 9.75m long and 3.5m wide (32 by 11.5ft). Tree-ring dating shows that it was built *c.* 1160–90, during the reign of Henry II, but as it had been broken up for its timbers to be included in a waterfront a century later the vessel had clearly been in use for a long time, through the reigns of Richard I and John.

The Cog

The type of seagoing ship known as a 'Cog' was an important cargo carrier in medieval England. It is shown on many seals of thirteenth- and fourteenth-century Germanic ports, such as Elbing, Damme, Stavoren, Danzig, Stralsund and Kiel, and was the major trading vessel of the Hanseatic League. Its most obvious characteristics were its straight stem- and stern-posts that angled upwards from the ends of a

48 Plan of wreck of the *Grace Dieu* in the River Hamble. (Copyright: National Maritime Museum, Greenwich)

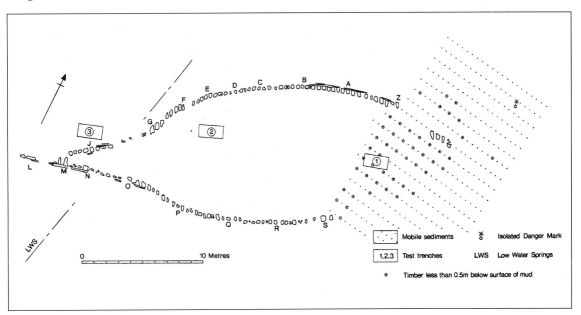

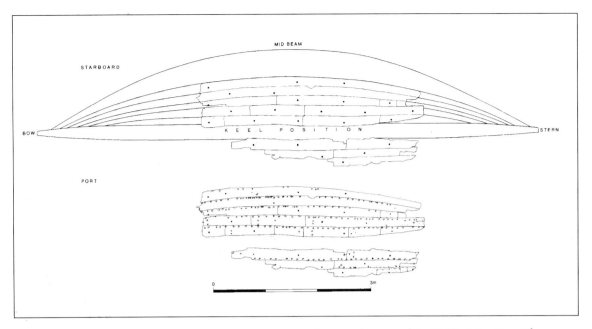

49 Suggested minimum reconstruction of Custom House boat. (Museum of London)

long straight keel. Fortunately it is not necessary to rely upon the seals to know how these vessels were built and used, for major parts of a number of Cogs have been found in the Low Countries and Scandinavia. The best-preserved dates from about 1380 and was discovered in the River Weser at Bremen in 1962. Since then it has been raised and restored at the maritime museum at Bremerhaven. It was 23.5m long, 7.8m wide and almost 5m deep (72 by 25 by 16ft), with clinker built sides and a carvel built bottom with an extra-thick plank as a keel. Instead of having rivets as clinker plank fastenings there were hooked iron nails that were driven through the planking from outboard and then were bent over inboard so that the point was embedded. Between the planks was a caulking of moss which was held by butterfly-shaped iron clamps.

Cogs were common in medieval English ports like Southampton and London, especially during the thirteenth and fourteenth centuries. For example, in 1224 the Southampton merchant Walter le Fleming sent his Cog *La Heitee* to La Rochelle to return with a cargo of wine, salt and other produce, and in 1350–4 *Le Cog Thomas de la Tour* carried wine from Bordeaux to London. Illustrations of Cogs in England are rare, though one is on the seal of the Priory of St Bartholomew in London. It is attached to a charter of 1533 but its style is thirteenth-century. Curiously, the ship is shown carrying a church, presumably because miracles apparently occurred at the Priory to merchants and sailors who had been saved from shipwreck by prayers or vows to the saint. Although no hulls of Cogs have yet been found in Britain, an almost complete fifteenth-century rudder that perhaps comes from one has been trawled up from the English Channel off Rye, and from this the shape and size of the ship's stern can be reconstructed (see **51**).

Information on English maritime trade during the medieval period is not restricted to discoveries in British waters, for at Vejby in eastern Denmark, by the straits between Denmark and Sweden, is the wreck of a late fourteenth-century Cog which had evidently traded with England. It had been driven onto the shore on a voyage home, and amongst the debris were 110 English gold nobles mostly of Edward III (1327–77), and 18 tonnes of ballast stones probably originating in Cornwall or Brittany.

1 Dover boat, Bronze Age. (Copyright: Canterbury Archaeological Trust)

2 Blackfriars ship 1, Romano-Celtic, second century AD

3 Roman lighthouse at Dover

4 Graveney boat, Saxon

5 Winchester font, showing a 'hulc'

6 East Watergate, London, a fourteenth-century dock

7 Blackfriars ship 3, a fifteenth-century barge from the River Thames

8 Spraying the raised warship *Mary Rose*, sunk in the Solent in 1545

9 Silver ducatons from the Dutch East Indiaman *Hollandia*, sunk in the Isles of Scilly, 1743

10 The Dutch East Indiaman *Amsterdam*, sunk near Hastings in 1749.
The bottom of the ship lies at a depth of about 8m (26ft)

11 Bottle of French red wine from the *Amsterdam*. Although sunk in the beach near Hastings
in 1749, when the wine was brought ashore from an archaeological excavation it still had
to pass through Customs entry at Newhaven

The Hulc

Medieval documentary records show that the Hulc was important in north European trade, the earliest known historical mention of such a vessel dating from about 1000 when it paid a toll of fourpence to berth at Billingsgate, London. But its appearance is based upon an interpretation of the seal of New Shoreham, used in 1295, which depicts a banana-shaped clinker built vessel and a surrounding inscription indicating that it was a Hulc (50). The image is far from clear, but at each end of the ship is a little castle, and at the stern on the port side there is a side rudder. Amidships there is a mast and yard for a square sail. The curved shape of the ship has undoubtedly been exaggerated to fit into the shape of the seal, though somewhat similar curved ships are depicted elsewhere where there were no restrictions, as on the twelfth-century font at Winchester Cathedral (**colour plate 5**), so the Hulc may indeed have had a considerable curvature.

From side rudder to sternpost rudder

The invention of the sternpost rudder, replacing the side rudder that had been used in Europe for at least 2000 years, was an extremely important thirteenth-century development because as ships became larger it became more difficult to control them with just one or possibly two fastenings to the hull, particularly when sailing into the wind or when the ship was heeled.

The difficulty of control can be imagined by studying an enormous oak side rudder dated to about 1200 which was trawled up from the English Channel off Rye (**51**). It is 6.7m (22ft) long (but was a little longer originally), with a blade 1.07m (3.5ft) wide at the bottom, and it weighed about half a tonne. Its forward edge is sharp and the trailing edge is broad and squared, so it must have created a great deal of drag as the water eddied behind its trailing edge, and these eddies may be the reason why this and other medieval rudders normally had a 'foot' shaped lower trailing edge – as if to feed off the

50 Seal of New Shoreham depicting a Hulc. (Copyright: Museum of London)

turbulence. Together with another rudder from Bergen, Norway, this is the largest side rudder known in medieval Europe, though it is unlike other medieval side rudders for it has no hole to fasten it to the hull indicating that it is unlikely that it was ever used. Perhaps it was washed out to sea from a shipyard at Rye or Winchelsea. But what type of ship it was intended for is far from clear, for it must have been for a vessel rather higher than the ships of Scandinavian type whose side rudders found at Bergen were only up to 4.46m (14.5ft) long. Perhaps it was a Cog or a Hulc.

The solution to obtaining better steering control was to mount the rudder onto the sternpost with several pintle and gudgeon iron fastenings, and it is this that came into general use during the thirteenth century. It seems to have been a north European invention for the earliest sternpost rudders are shown on a number of port seals, such as Elbing (*c.* 1242) and Wismar (1256) in Germany, and Poole (1325), Rye (*c.* 1390) and Tenterden (*c.* 1449) in southern England. An almost complete sternpost rudder of the fifteenth century has been trawled up from the Channel off Rye, and

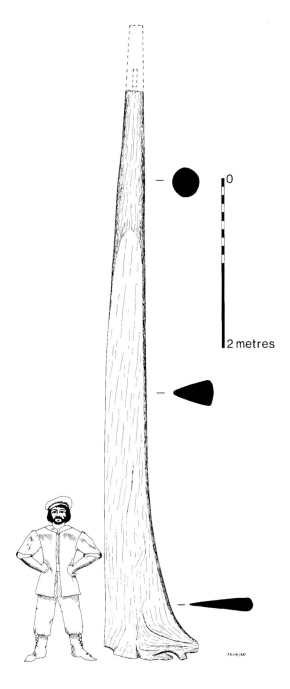

0

2 metres

51 Rye side rudder, *c.* 1200.

the remains of the three wrought iron pintles which originally slotted into gudgeons in the sternpost. What is interesting is that this rudder has flat parallel sides which probably created less drag than did the side rudder, suggesting that there was a growing understanding of hydrodynamic shapes.

Several masts

Until the fifteenth century all sailing ships in northern waters had only one mast and one square sail, but as vessels became larger it was increasingly difficult to handle and adjust very large single sails to give the best balance for propulsion. Sail area could be made smaller by reefing as is shown in ships depicted on some thirteenth-century port seals, but eventually it became more convenient to distribute the sailing force among a number of sails located on several masts along the ship, including a head sail mounted on the bowsprit. Moreover, the ability to sail into the wind was aided by adding a fore-and-aft sail, somewhat as had long been used by Arabs in the Mediterranean, though this was placed on the after or mizzen mast. These improved sailing arrangements took some time to perfect, and from an early date they were used on a particularly important type of ship, the Carrack, which initially in the fourteenth century carried two masts, but by the fifteenth century had a third mast. For a while experiments were made giving ships four masts in addition to a bowsprit with a sail, but this was found to be excessive and in due course the three-master became normal in Europe. The mainsail and the foresail were the driving sails, with the bowsprit sail as a headsail to keep the bow off the wind.

Since the purpose of the after sail, the mizzen, was to help with steering, and the foresail helped to balance the ship on the wind, the position of the main mast and its sails was particularly important in driving the ship. Consequently it is very important to record accurately the position of any mast-steps in wrecks, particularly in relation to the total

judging from the height of the tiller fastening, the stern of the vessel was at least 4.5m (14.75ft) high. The shape of the bottom of the rudder shows that the sternpost had been inclined at an angle to the keel, and there were length of the keel. One of the earliest known two- or possibly three-masted English ships was Henry V's warship *Grace Dieu*, of 1400 'tuns', completed in 1418, whose bottom is believed to have survived in the Hamble River at Bursledon, near Southampton (see **5** and **48**). This vessel only served in one naval event when it was part of a 'sea-keeping patrol' off Southampton in 1420 under the Earl of Devonshire, but unfortunately some of its crew mutinied and forced its master to put into St Helens, Isle of Wight. By December that year it was moored in the River Hamble with a skeleton crew, and there it remained until 7 January 1439, when 'about the middle of the night' the ship was struck by lightning during a storm and caught fire. Afterwards it was broken up.

The wreck is about 35.5m long and 11.2m wide (116 by 37ft), but it is estimated that the complete ship was at least 40m long and 15m wide. The junction of the stempost and keel has been found, and above the keel is the keelson in which there is the socket for the base of the main mast. But as this measured only 58cm (2ft) by 29cm (1ft) it must have taken a tenon at the base of the mast, for the great mast itself was recorded originally as being about 2m (6.5ft) in circumference at deck level. Although it is not easy to relate the mast position exactly to the rest of the hull, it appears to have been located well forward of the widest part of the ship, leaving room for a mizzen mast with a lateen sail near the stern.

The enormous size of the vessel gave the shipwrights special problems in achieving a strong watertight hull. The oak ribs, about 28 by 20cm (12 by 7in) in section, were close together and fastened to the planking by oak trenails, but it was the outboard planking that gave special strength, for, although clinker built and fastened with thousands of large iron rivets, each plank comprised a sandwich of three layers of wood giving a total thickness of about 15cm (6in), with a caulking of moss and tar. Inboard there was a further strengthening of planks (a 'ceiling') and longitudinal inner beams ('stringers').

What this wreck shows is that clinker shipbuilding in the largest vessels had become so complex and wasteful of materials that it was necessary to find an alternative method of building. The solution in northern Europe, developed in warships at the beginning of the sixteenth century, was to build them with carvel laid (edge-to-edge) planks as were ships in the Mediterranean, but this meant building ships in a fundamentally different way. Only then would northern European vessels undertake the greatest voyages of discovery to America, the Far East, and even around the world. Awareness of the Far East already existed, as is shown by a fragment of a Japanese bronze bell from a fourteenth-century waterfront deposit in London. But what Londoners made of its strange engraved script can only be imagined, though it does show that there was a demand for Far Eastern goods at that early date even though they had to be brought by land along the 'silk road'. One day, in the sixteenth century, ships would carry valuable cargoes by sea from Asia to England.

Cargoes

There is an enormous amount of documentary and archaeological information relating to English medieval trade and to the cargoes that the ships carried. Manuscript records show that for each voyage there was an agreement, drawn up by a public notary, between the merchant who wanted to charter a ship and the master of the vessel. The agreement dealt with the cargo, the freight charge, the destination, and the payment of dues and other costs such as pilotage and port customs. Wine carried in tuns or barrels in due course became 'tonnage', the measure of a ship's capacity.

Clues to the variety of goods carried also exist in archaeological remains, though documentary records often mention things that are not found. For example, customs payment was due from ships using the public wharf of Billingsgate, London, on such goods as corn, sea-coal, ale, fish, butter, leather, nuts, honey, lead, iron, wine, onions, garlic, clay and potter's earth 'imported and exported', boards called 'weynscotte' and 'ryghholt', flax, feathers and litmus. The customs add that 'for pottery imported, that is to say, tureens, pipkins, patens, earthen pots . . . the said bailiff shall take nothing'. As far as fish were concerned other customs were very specific. At Queenhithe, London, it was decreed 'that no boat that brings oysters, whelks, mussels or soles, shall remain longer upon sale than one high tide and two ebbs. And whosoever shall lie a longer time, as for his oysters, whelks or mussels, let them be forfeited.' Presumably this was to ensure that customers received only fresh fish.

Archaeology enables many of such objects, like the pottery and the barrels of wine, to be visualized, and by studying the distribution of traded objects it also preserves evidence of voyages some of which are not referred to in documentary records. This even includes objects found in medieval ports that should not normally be found there but must have been brought by ship. For example, although the port of Dublin was founded in the ninth century by Vikings, a few pieces of Roman samian ware of the first and second centuries AD have been noted in the medieval deposits and were perhaps brought from England. Also, a second-century AD Roman coin has been found in early medieval deposits at Bergen, founded in 1070. These may well have arrived in the ballast, sand and gravel dredged from river beds and placed in medieval ships at early ports such as York and London.

Ports

Since voyages were arranged, started and finished at ports, and cargoes were bought and sold there, the port facilities are of fundamental importance to understanding medieval trade, ships and seafaring. The most extensively excavated medieval port waterfront in Britain is at London where the pattern changed from 'horizontal' berthing on prepared tidal beaches

in the eleventh and twelfth centuries, to 'vertical' berthing at fourteenth- and fifteenth-century quays and docks. Behind the quays were warehouses, the homes of merchants and financiers, and the market places, the study of which are as necessary as the investigation of shipwrecks.

In London, however, excavations have concentrated on the early medieval waterfronts, so comparatively limited attention has been given to the later medieval quays. But for later medieval periods there exists a considerable amount of documentary evidence to help with their interpretation, particularly the traditional customs of London which are recorded in a fifteenth-century book compiled from miscellaneous archives dating back to the twelfth and thirteenth centuries. These include the regulation of shipping and the fishing industry; the fixing of mooring-posts in the river; the removal of weirs and other obstructions; the cleansing of the river; directing the removal of ballast for ships from the river bed; the licensing of wharves, jetties, mills, etc.; and the erection and maintenance of public stairs and landing places.

The only extensively excavated public quay in Britain is a fourteenth-century dock with stone walls called East Watergate in London. It was 11m wide and 36m long (36 by 118ft), and was served at its landward end by the junction of two streets (**52**, **53** and **colour plate 6**). At its mouth was a mooring post, and on either side of the dock were quays with timber rubbing posts up to 3m (10ft) apart to protect boats from damage on the stones, and at one point a timber loading platform projected out over the water. The types of vessels using the East Watergate are referred to in a fourteenth-century dispute arising from a building encroachment into the dock 'to the nuisance of ships (*navium*), shouts (*shoutarum*) and boats (*batellorum*) putting in there'. On one side was a broad gravelled quayside area where cargoes could be piled, and behind that were the remains of an arcaded warehouse.

The larger ships could not reach the public quays so it was necessary for them to moor in the stream, and in London a fifteenth-century mooring site off Billingsgate is indicated by the broken fluke of a large wrought-iron anchor. Such river moorings were sometimes marked by buoys.

Shipbuilding and repairing were essential industries at ports, and these leave useful evidence of intermediate stages in construction methods. For example at Perth strips of unused wrought-iron roves for rivets indicate boatbuilding took place nearby in the twelfth century. And at Poole a shipwright's store comprising stacks of over sixty roughly shaped ribs and stemposts were found where they were left about 1500 or a little earlier so as to season in the tidal sands at the waterfront.

The river beds at historic ports are always strewn with the rubbish and accidental losses from ships, and one of the most important recent finds is that of a medieval bronze trumpet from a

52 Medieval waterfront, City of London, typical of many sites from the twelfth to the fifteenth century. (Copyright: Museum of London)

fourteenth-century riverbed deposit in London. It was found dismantled into several sections, as if it had been dropped overboard by accident, but when put together it was about 1.7m (5.5ft) long, though of fairly light weight. This was probably used on board ship by the master standing at the stern as a means of giving orders to the crew as they clambered aloft to set sail. The use of similar trumpets at the start of voyages during the thirteenth and fourteenth centuries is shown on the seals of Great Yarmouth (*c.* 1280), Pevensey (early thirteenth-century), Winchelsea (thirteenth-century), Lydd (early fourteenth-century), Dover (1305), Hythe (late thirteenth-century) and Faversham (late thirteenth-century).

Since trumpets were rather unwieldy they appear to have been replaced later by bugles as well as by the smaller and more convenient

53 Artist's impression of the fourteenth-century East Watergate, London. (Copyright: Museum of London)

'boatswain's pipe'. By the fifteenth century the pipes were being replicated in pewter as souvenirs for pilgrims who crossed the sea. These too have been found in the Thames at London and are very similar to modern boatswain's whistles of brass and silver.

Boats on inland waters

Whilst the major developments were taking place in large ships, most other smaller vessels were used for local coastal and inland water transportation and probably remained relatively unchanged. Dugout boats continued to be used as small personal vessels, like the box-shaped craft recovered from the River Thames at Kew

that has been dated by carbon 14 to the thirteenth century. It was about 4.42m (14.5ft) long and 0.76m (2.5ft) wide, with squared ends and had a bulkhead across the middle. A hydrostatic study shows that it could have carried two men and a quarter of a tonne of goods, with a freeboard of 0.41m (1.3ft). Another boat, found in the former Lake Kentmere, Westmorland, was more unusual in that the dugout oak bottom had its sides extended upwards with planks attached clinkerwise to four small ribs. It is carbon 14 dated to the thirteenth or fourteenth century, and was originally about 4.25m long, 0.85m wide and 0.6m deep (14 by 2.75 by 2ft), with a seat for an oarsman near the middle and beside that a well-worn rowlock hole in the planking. At the bow and stern were seats for passengers.

Medieval documentary records show that there were many types of river craft with strange names, such as Bark, Chalkboat, Cockboat, Dungboat, Farcost, Ferryboat, Float, Flune, Hakeboat, Keel, Ketch, Lighter, Mangboat, Oysterboat, Piker, Rushboat, Shout, Spindlersboat, Tideboat and Whelkboat. These existed on the River Thames, and other rivers no doubt had some alternative regional names. But as most of these refer to their use there is no clue to how much variety of form and construction was represented. Indeed, if the many fragments of medieval boats found in London are representative of such a broad range of vessels, then it seems that during the medieval period they were all of oak and were all clinker built with iron rivets and hair caulking. Fragments of boats have also been found at other medieval ports of Lincoln, York and Dublin, as well as at Magor Pill in south Wales, all with the same construction. A substantial part of a similar boat of the thirteenth century was found in the River Severn at Magor Pill, south Wales. It was wrecked apparently while

carrying a cargo of iron ore. However, it is important to remember that clinker planking with iron rivets is immediately recognizable in an excavation as having come from a boat, and it is possible that carvel built local boats existed, perhaps continuing the Celtic tradition of shipbuilding, but their fragments have still to be identified.

The most complete and best studied medieval plank-built river vessel yet found in Britain is a fifteenth-century barge discovered as a wreck in the River Thames at Blackfriars, London (Blackfriars ship 3) in 1970 (**54–57** and **colour plate** 7). Its distinctive characteristics matched those of a very common type of medieval river barge known as a Shout. It had been built, according to the tree-ring study, probably between 1380 and 1415, and had been sunk, judging from pottery found in the wreck, probably about 1480–1500. It was about 14.64m long, 4.3m wide and 0.88m deep amidships (48 by 14 by 3ft), and was of oak, clinker built and

54 General view from bow of Blackfriars ship 3.

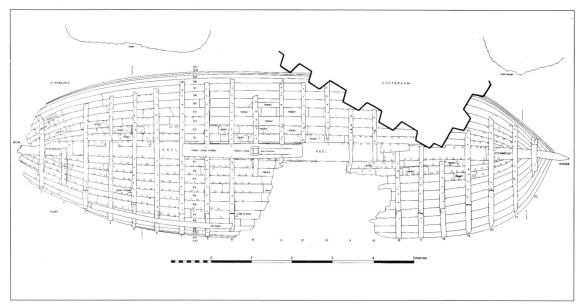

55 Plan and cross-profiles of Blackfriars ship 3. (Copyright: Museum of London)

56 Stern end of Blackfriars ship 3.

57 Reconstruction drawing of Blackfriars ship 3.
(Copyright: Museum of London)

sharp at both ends, with a mast just forward of amidships, which, in this position, would have carried a square sail. The barge had evidently frequently passed under bridges for its mast had been unstepped and its foot slid aft so often that a hollow had been worn in the mast-step timber. As there were no fittings for a rudder at the stern it was most likely guided by a large steering oar. A hydrostatic analysis shows that the barge could carry a cargo of about 7.5 tonnes at a waterline of 0.4m (1.3ft).

The London documentary records of Shouts are extensive, and show that they could be built by four or five men in about three weeks, and that some were probably built at riverside boatyards in the medieval maritime 'quarter' just west of the Tower of London. The detail of the records is remarkable for they even note that on the completion of a vessel there was normally a celebration, as in 1406–7 when beer was bought 'and given to the men around the launching of the Shout in the Thames on the said Saturday'.

6
Sixteenth-century seafarers

When one looks at the sixteenth-century warship *Mary Rose* in its fine museum at Portsmouth, it is clear how large and complex ships had become since the earliest known plank-built boats almost 3000 years earlier. By now the largest ships were more than mobile buildings and had become floating villages, for in a statement of 1545 it was said that the *Mary Rose* was home to 700 men. This ship was exceptional, however, for she was created by a Tudor monarch whose reign was characterized by a growth in English independence from Europe and a break with the Church of Rome. She was part of England's first permanent navy defending the nation and its expanding trade following the voyages of global discovery and settlement in the wake of the Spanish and Portuguese explorers who, during the 1490s, had found America and the sea route around the Cape to the Far East.

At the start of the sixteenth century English trade was mainly with countries around the North Sea, with cloth a particularly important export. By the middle of the century trade had been extended to Russia, with furs, timber and pitch being imported; and during the latter half of the century amazing voyages by Englishmen took place: Hawkins sailed to Porto Rico, Florida and Sierra Leone; Frobisher went to Hudson's Bay; Gilbert to Newfoundland; Fitch to Syria; Lancaster sailed to the East; Raleigh tried to discover Eldorado up the Orinoco; Adams settled in Japan; and Drake and Cavendish circumnavigated the globe. The result was to stimulate the English to consider maritime success as the means of securing commercial success abroad. London had become the headquarters of a range of organizations trading with distant lands, such as the Turkey and Africa Companies, and in 1600 the East India Company.

This expansion of maritime activity created a growing understanding of the design and construction of ships, and from the late sixteenth century the first written descriptions of the theory of ship design, construction and how sailing ships behave when afloat exist. Moreover, there were major developments in the administration of maritime trade and the navy.

Armed trading ships

The wrecks of sixteenth-century merchant ships from the Mediterranean as well as from the north have been found on the seabed around Britain (58). Many of these larger vessels were armed, since piracy was still endemic in European waters in spite of the existence of growing navies. Some pirates even had the audacity to carry their activities into rivers, such as in 1526 when two ships were 'taken awaye, robbed and dispoyled on the Ryver of Tamyse by certeyn pyrotts', and two years later a French warship and a Flemish vessel had a running fight all the way up the Thames to Tower Wharf in the port of London.

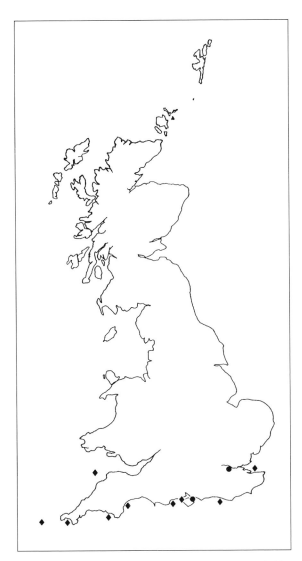

58 Map of sixteenth-century excavated wrecks recorded in Great Britain. ●= warships; ◆= armed merchantmen.

in 1847 on the Girdler Sand, off Whitstable, may be typical of many losses that are at present only known from documentary records. It had iron guns and stone shot, and was carrying a cargo that included over 2700 ingots, possibly of tin, one of which was stamped with the royal mark of a rose surmounted by a crown suggesting that it was English. Also there was some iron, lead in pigs, and red lead apparently in cast-iron casks covered in wood. A doublet of a kind that was in fashion at the time of Elizabeth I suggests that the wreck occurred in the latter half of the sixteenth century.

The wrecks of several other early armed merchantmen have been found which are likely to be of the sixteenth century, though a fifteenth-century date is also sometimes possible. One may be the *St Anthony*, a Portuguese merchantman, which was found in Mounts Bay, Cornwall. If correctly identified, that ship sank in 1527 on a voyage from Lisbon to Antwerp with a mixed cargo, much of which was salvaged at the time, though in the wreck silver and copper ingots have been recovered recently. Another wreck, on Church Rocks, Teignmouth, Devon, included several bronze guns that had been manufactured in Italy in the sixteenth century suggesting that this was also a Mediterranean ship. Six guns of bronze and wrought iron of the sixteenth century were found on the seabed at Brighton Marina and mark the site of an unidentified vessel, presumably an armed merchant ship. A wrought-iron gun, two iron breech blocks and some stone shot mark the site of yet another off Gull Rock, Lundy Island, Devon. Another armed ship, possibly the *San Bartolome*, a Spanish ship wrecked in 1597, has been found on Bartholomew Ledge, Isles of Scilly. In it was metal scrap in the form of broken bronze bells, and many lead ingots. Unfortunately little information about any of these wrecks has been published, even though some are protected as historic sites, so it is not possible to compare and analyse them. At least they show that important detailed archaeological information

But piracy was not the only problem, for poor navigation also led to ships running aground, even when vessels were being guided by pilots whose job was then often termed 'loadmanage' (from 'load' meaning journey – as in loadstone, and 'manage' meaning to handle a ship). There are many documented losses, particularly in the estuaries of rivers leading to ports when landmarks and seamarks were obscured. The Thames estuary and the Goodwin Sands off eastern Kent were particularly dangerous, and a sixteenth-century wreck found about sixteenth-century merchant ships can be found. Other possible sixteenth-century wreck sites are indicated by the recoveries of wrought-iron guns from the sea off Lowestoft, Harwich, Pevensey and Dover, and the discovery of a sixteenth-century Portuguese bronze swivel gun, 2.38m (11ft) long, with an iron handle and swivel, near the Goodwin Sands.

One wreck that is being carefully studied is that of an armed Spanish merchant vessel that sank in Studland Bay, off Poole, Dorset, probably during the 1520s. Its carvel built bottom lay in one spot, and 50m (164ft) away was a large part of its collapsed starboard side which included possible deck fittings and scuppers, one of which had been blocked with a wooden bung. The junction of the keel and the sternpost was found, together with iron fittings for a rudder. The pottery included mainly Spanish wares, particularly decorated Spanish tin-glazed polychrome and Maiolica lustreware, which are rarely found in England. There was also a little Portuguese and French pottery. There were at least 1.4 tonnes of stone ballast, 55 per cent of which is from the Basque coast indicating its possible place of origin. Life on board is suggested by various personal possessions, and butchered bones indicate that the crew ate salt beef, mutton and pork. Seeds indicate that wheat, pepper and figs were part of their diet, and a rotary quern shows that grain was milled, presumably for fresh bread to be baked on board. Its armament included two wrought-iron guns which have been recovered, one a large breech loader for use on deck and the other a swivel gun for firing stone shot, but there was also some shot of other sizes which implies that other guns were on board.

Yet another foreign ship, dating from the mid-sixteenth century, has been found off Yarmouth, Isle of Wight. A substantial amount of the ship's structure remains, and it too was carvel built and fastened largely with iron nails. The pottery found suggests a Mediterranean origin, perhaps Venetian, though other objects from England and the Low Countries indicate a fairly wide range in its pattern of trade. A bronze gun with the initials ZA, probably made by Zuane Alberghetti of Italy, was found with the remains of a long, low, wooden gun carriage.

Part of the bottom of a probable English merchant ship, which sunk during the first half of the sixteenth century, has been studied in the Cattewater reach of the River Plym, at the port of Plymouth. This seems to have been an accidental loss since it is unlikely that its guns would have been abandoned deliberately. It had an oak keel, and its ribs were fastened by trenails to oak carvel-laid planks. The planks had been sawn to shape and the vessel 'skeleton built', the planks having been fastened to the pre-erected framework of ribs. There was an inner skin or ceiling of oak and pine planks, and over the keel was an oak keelson containing a mast-step, a rectangular socket measuring 0.33m by 0.76m (1 by 2.5ft). Its three built-up iron swivel guns were probably mounted on the gunwale. The stone ballast, apparently derived from south-west England and south Wales, suggests that it was a fairly local coastal trader.

Ports

The merchantmen trading at many English ports found serious problems with customs' arrangements in the first half of the sixteenth century and these had an adverse effect on trade. The problem was that earlier medieval monarchs had restricted trade in the 'staples', or principal goods to specific places, and by the sixteenth century had not allowed for changes in places of production and in the location of ports. Moreover, some 'head ports' like Chester, where customs were collected, had declined, whereas some subsidiary 'member ports' and even 'creeks' had grown to become important in their own right even though convenient arrangements for collecting customs had not been brought up to date. The reasons for decline were various, such as shifts in trade as at Southampton and Milford Haven, while other ports suffered from silting as at Chester, Orford,

King's Lynn and at the Cinque ports of Rye, Winchelsea and Pevensey. Conversely, the port of Dunwich, Suffolk, and Hastings, Sussex, were being eroded away by the sea. Some up-river locations for certain old ports were found to be inconvenient, and were superseded by new ports downstream, such as Yarmouth replacing Norwich, Boston replacing Lincoln, and Hull replacing York. But other ports did survive, particularly Bristol in the west and London in the east.

The difficulties were compounded by London, which was, for customs' purposes, the main port in England with all other ports termed 'outports'. London was ideally placed for political and trading links with the Continent, and was the power base of merchants who sought to control much of the trade and wealth of England for their benefit. The result was that in 1558 the Crown examined the problem and issued a new list of ports where trade could legally occur, and this did much to hasten the decline of some ports and encouraged the growth of others.

The archaeological study of the changing fortunes of many ports during the medieval period and the sixteenth century is possible through excavation and would be of enormous value in reconstructing what they were like. So far the few waterfront excavations that have taken place at ports in Britain have concentrated on the Roman and earlier medieval phases, with the result that we know less about their archaeology in the sixteenth century.

There is one sixteenth-century seaport, however, for which an archaeological record has been made, and that was in Hastings as long ago as 1833. A recently identified survey made then of ancient pile foundations and stones in the beach in front of the medieval town shows that the port was protected by a sea wall about 6m (20ft) thick, and that at one end there was a stone pier about 15m (50ft) wide jutting out about 30m (100ft) into the sea. This apparently dated from before 1578, and was designed to allow a gravel beach to form on the west side of the pier while creating a protected tidal beach on the leeward east side for merchant vessels to load and unload at low tide. There were also extra pile foundations which seem to date from a documented strengthening in 1595 when the sea wall was increased to 9m (30ft) thick, and the pier became about 26m (85ft) thick. A contemporary account says that the pier was 9m (30ft) high. But even this massive structure was not strong enough to withstand the force of the seas for it was badly damaged in storms in 1597, and although repaired it was finally destroyed in a storm in 1656. To this day the scattered rocks of the sea wall and pier are known as 'Pier Rocks'.

Coastal and river vessels

A few fragments of the once numerous small vessels that carried food, building materials and other supplies around the coast and along the inland waterways of sixteenth-century Britain have been discovered, and, not surprisingly, all are clinker built as if these small local traditional vessels were slow to change to carvel construction. But other changes were occurring among even those local vessels. In London the pieces of local boats found reused in waterfront revetments show that there was an increasing use of elm planking instead of oak, and that planks were often tangentially sawn, whereas previously they had only been radially split from the log. There was also a decline in the quality of shipbuilding materials, the elm being more knotty and with a wider grain than the oak, perhaps reflecting the reducing availability of suitable oak trees. One find of particular interest was part of the stern of a boat built about 1580 which had been constructed in 'reverse clinker', each lower plank overlapping the upper outboard (59). This was probably a specialized vessel such as a Dungboat since it was apparently easier to shovel out such a 'cargo' from a reverse clinker vessel than from a conventional clinker craft. Other changes were found in the type of caulking materials of the London boat fragments, wool and cattle hair

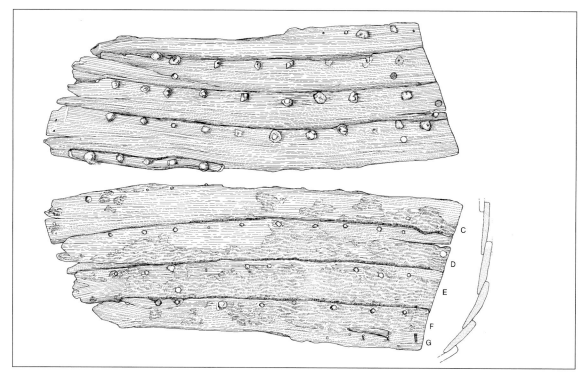

59 Reverse clinker boat. (Copyright: Museum of London)

being mostly used in the sixteenth century instead of the goat hair used earlier.

Moss was not a caulking material in the sixteenth-century London boat fragments, and yet it was used in the most complete small ship of the sixteenth century found in Britain. This suggests that it was a foreign vessel, even though it had sunk in an old bed of the River Rother near Rye, Sussex. It was discovered in 1822, and was 19.4m long, 4.57m wide, 1.67m high amidships (63.75 by 15 by 5.5ft), and sharp at both ends. At each end was a small cabin, and between them was a large hold much of which was originally covered with an arched timber roof (**60, 61**). The vessel lay buried in 3m (10ft) of 'sea sand' with several great baulks of timber, one 12m long and 0.55m square (39 by 2ft), attesting to a violent and catastrophic inundation. The vessel had a hole stove through its bottom forward, and the foremost part of its keel was missing. The suddenness of the tragedy became clear as the after cabin was excavated, for here were two human skeletons, one an

adult and the other a child. The partly charred cinders on the hearth showed that the fire had been extinguished suddenly. Outside the ship was more evidence of the tragedy, for there the excavators found another human skeleton, together with the skeleton of a dog resembling a greyhound. It seems that a small family with their pet dog had suddenly been engulfed.

The small ship was built from oak throughout, and it had a flat bottom of carvel-laid planks, but the sides which angled sharply upwards were clinker built with three broad strakes. Oak trenails, wedged at both ends, fastened the planks and an inner ceiling of planks to the ribs. The outer clinker planking was fastened together with iron rivets, and had a caulking of moss. The mast-step lay one-third of the length from the bow, and in this position the missing mast no doubt carried a fore-and-aft sail. A large rudder at the stern was apparently not operated by a tiller but instead by ropes worked from a 'dumb-roller' mounted on a beam over the after deck.

A number of objects found in the wreck point to a date in the first half of the sixteenth

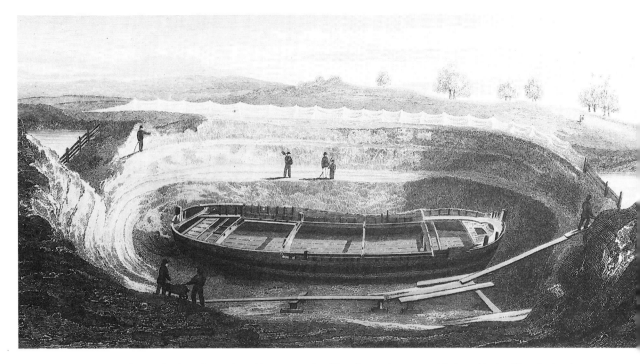

60 Ship found in bed of River Rother. (Reproduced by courtesy of the Society of Antiquaries of London)

61 The sixteenth-century ship found in the River Rother in 1822. (Redrawn from records by William McPherson Rice, preserved at the National Maritime Museum)

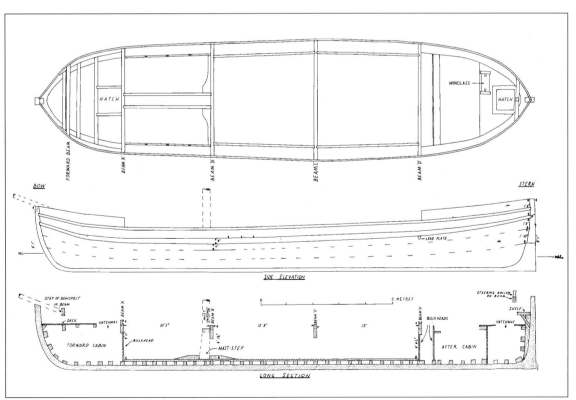

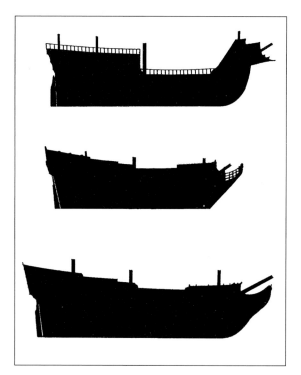

62 The development of English warships, not to scale. (Top) the Carrack *Mary Rose* (sunk 1545); (middle) the 70-gun warship *Anne* (sunk 1690); (bottom) HMS *Victory* (about 1800).

century: several pottery cooking utensils near the hearth in the after cabin, an ink horn, a brass pin, a steel and flint for making fire, a whetstone, the locks from wooden lockers and decorated floor tiles used in the hearth. The sounding lead indicates that it was a seagoing ship, and as the vessel is so similar to Dutch wrecks found in the Netherlands, and much of the pottery on board seems to have been Dutch, it is likely that it was a small Dutch coastal trading vessel.

There is a curious postscript to the story of this vessel, for after excavation it was floated and eventually brought to London for public exhibition in the Waterloo Road. But public interest declined and the vessel was broken up. One trenail, however, was saved by a local collector, Syer Cuming, and is still supposed to be in the museum he founded in Southwark. Sadly, that trenail too is now missing.

The Navy

The threat of invasion by France and Spain and the need to protect England's developing trade and sea routes made it necessary for Henry VII and Henry VIII to establish a permanent navy. During the medieval period monarchs had built warships from time to time, such as the *Grace Dieu*, and at times had pressed merchantmen into service, but it was not until the latter half of the fifteenth century that guns became such an important part of a warship that changes in hull design and construction began to occur. There were several types of sixteenth-century warship, such as the Galleass, a large, oared sailing vessel, but the main type was the Carrack, a three- or four-masted vessel, square-rigged on fore and main masts and lateen-rigged on the mizzen (**62**). The Carrack was characterized by high fore and after castles, and a deep waist between, with the forecastle overhanging the bow. Its guns were mostly located on the main decks, with lighter guns on the castles. There are contemporary sixteenth-century pictures of such vessels, one of the most important sources being the Anthony Roll, an illustrated list of Henry VIII's warships completed in 1546. This document shows that they were decorated with painted geometric designs, and that hanging from the bowsprit of each was a great iron grappling hook ready to be dropped onto an enemy ship so that the two vessels could be drawn together enabling hand fighting to ensue.

When Henry VII, first of the Tudor monarchs, came to the throne in 1485 he had to rely on hired merchantmen for naval purposes, but quickly he started building warships, the largest of which were the Carracks *Sovereign*, 800 tons and with three masts, and the *Regent*, with four masts and 1000 tons. These were completed in 1488, and had clinker planking, which meant that their main armament of guns had to be on the open upper deck since it was not easy to cut gunports through such a hull without weakening the ship. It soon became clear that in at least the larger ships the clinker planking should be replaced by the stronger and less wasteful carvel planking as was used in the Mediterranean ships.

The change from clinker to carvel apparently dates from about 1509, for in that year the *Sovereign* was rebuilt with carvel planking after the clinker had been removed, and the *Mary Rose*, a new ship, was built at Portsmouth with carvel planks from its inception. A valuable clue to how the rebuilding was achieved is shown by the discovery in 1912 of the bottom of an enormous ship at Woolwich, beside the River Thames downstream from London (**63**). It is believed to be Henry VII's *Sovereign*, which had been abandoned in a decaying state in a dock at Woolwich by 1521. When found it was carvel planked, but the ribs still retained traces of the 'steps' from the earlier clinker construction. Unfortunately no contemporary picture exists of the *Sovereign*.

63 The Woolwich ship, probably Henry VII's warship *Sovereign*, found in 1912 at Woolwich Power Station. (Copyright: Corporation of London)

The remains of the Woolwich ship were impressive, as befitted a floating castle, for it was built of oak and had a rounded bottom cross-section amidships indicating that originally it had a beam of at least 13.7m (45ft). Although the remains uncovered were 29m (95ft) long and incomplete, it seems likely that the keel was originally about 36m (118ft) long, and that the whole ship had a total length of very roughly 45m (147ft). The hull was extremely strong, with a keel 0.53m wide and 0.33m deep (1.75 by 1ft), and outer planks, 0.1m (4in) thick, which were attached by trenails to substantial ribs 0.35m wide, 0.2m deep and spaced 0.12m apart (1ft by 7in by 4in), inboard of which was a ceiling of planks about 0.07m (3in) thick. The seams between the outer planks were caulked with pitch and oakum and were covered outboard by battens of wood. The hull was further strengthened inboard by massive secondary frames, riders and stringers.

The lower 2m (6.5ft) of the mast itself had survived in about the middle of the ship, and was built from a central spine of wood around which were eight timbers which thickened it to a diameter of 1.32m (4.3ft). This whole massive structure was held together with iron bands. The bottom of the mast had a tenon which was set in a wooden mast-step or socket 0.71m (2.3ft) wide.

The rebuilding of the *Sovereign* had occurred immediately after Henry VIII came to the throne, as part of the modernization and enlargement of the English navy. This included placing more reliance on an armament of heavy guns as shown by documents which record that in 1495 the *Sovereign* was armed with 141 fairly light guns, but that after her rebuild in 1509 these were replaced by 84 heavier guns. Modernization continued, for the *Mary Rose* which initially included 7 heavy bronze guns and 34 heavy iron guns, was given 91 guns, 15 of which were of bronze, after her rebuild in 1536. Another important change was replacing the pointed stern of earlier ships with a squared one so that guns could be pointed aft, but

whether this occurred when the *Mary Rose* was built in 1509 or rebuilt in 1536 is not clear.

The discovery of the wreck of the *Mary Rose* in 1971, and its recovery in 1982, has led to enormous advances in understanding this important stage in naval development. It could be said that she was one of the first ships of the English navy to be built to carry guns as her main armament. The Anthony Roll of 1546 shows that she had four masts with square sails on her main and fore masts, and lateen sails on her two mizzen masts. This was her state on the eve of her loss in 1545 when, in an engagement with a French fleet in the Solent outside Portsmouth harbour, she capsized with the loss of most of her complement of mariners, soldiers and gunners. The reason for the capsize of this 36-year-old vessel is far from clear, but she sank into 12m (39ft) of water and, in a heeled state on the seabed, was soon partly enveloped in soft silts. This ensured the preservation of about one-third of the hull, mostly the starboard side where the hull survived to a height of up to 13m (42ft) (**64** and **colour plate 8**). From her remains it has been possible to reconstruct some of her approximate dimensions: a length of keel of 32m, a breadth of 11.4m, and a waterline length of 37.3m (105 by 37.5 by 122.3ft).

The accidental loss of the ship has ensured that examples of various guns have been preserved, the two main types being breech-loading and muzzle-loading. There was no standardization in the guns or their equipment and this must have made it difficult to service all the guns properly and then to fire them accurately. A tight-fitting shot could cause a weak gun to explode, whereas shot that was too small would lose much of the force of the gunpowder charge in 'windage'.

The breech-loaded guns were particularly primitive and dangerous to use by later standards, having been made mostly of lengths of wrought iron held together as a tube by iron bands, the whole gun being mounted on a wooden bed. They were fitted with a new breech-block containing a gunpowder charge

64 Detail of *Mary Rose.*

each time the gun was fired. The muzzle-loading bronze guns were safer and more modern for they were cast in one piece, the barrel having been bored. They were mounted on elm carriages to be run back for cleaning and reloading. The ship also carried many longbows and thousands of arrows for archers who were part of the ship's fighting force, but by 1545, when the *Mary Rose* sank, this medieval type of weapon was already being superseded by the hand gun, showing yet again that the ship was at an historical watershed in naval warfare.

The silts in which the ship lay also preserved evidence of the life on board. The skeletons of about 200 people were found, most being in their late teens and early twenties, and with them were traces of food, particularly butchered meat bones stored in barrels. Pewter plates, tankards and spoons were used by the officers, whilst the men used wooden tableware for their food, which was cooked in a huge cauldron supported by iron bars over a fire box in the hold just forward of the main mast. But life on board had its problems too, and traces of fleas and other insects, and the remains of a rat, were all found, and this infestation must have made life difficult in the dark, damp and cramped conditions. This was relieved by various recreations, games such as backgammon, playing various musical instruments, and reading books helped to pass the time away. An important individual was the barber surgeon, whose job was to look after the health of the crew. His small cabin was found on the main deck, and in it was a bench and a chest containing medical equipment.

The next stage in warship development occurred in the second half of the sixteenth century, when efforts were made to make ships more stable by reducing the height of the castles. The result was the Galleon, but although during the reign of Elizabeth I (1558–1603) some forty-seven ships were added to the Royal Navy, little detail is known about what they were like. The archaeological discovery of warship wrecks in the future should be able to add considerable information, and might show if their underwater shape was sleeker to give less resistance in the water. Moreover, the further developments in armament might be represented by discoveries of cast-iron guns that documentary records show generally replaced the more expensive bronze guns, and placed a greater reliance on longer-range broadside fire instead of boarding and hand fighting.

The construction, repair and servicing of naval ships had meant that dockyards were required, and it was Henry VII who ordered the construction of the first naval dry dock, built in 1496 at Portsmouth. This yard was enlarged by Henry VIII who created others at Chatham and Woolwich. The archaeological investigation of these and other British dockyards at home and abroad is still in its infancy, but it is important to remember that they are very important clues to the beginnings of England's permanent navy.

The Spanish Armada

The limited information about Elizabethan warships does not extend to vessels of King Philip II's Armada, whose attempt to invade England in 1588 caused the loss of so many Spanish ships and men. This was probably more to do with poor Spanish management than with the success of the English naval forces. The aim was to sail the fleet of 130 ships under the command of the Duke of Medina Sidonia from Lisbon into the English Channel and then to pick up the army of the Prince of Parma, but after twenty days it had to put into Corunna for repairs and provisions due to bad weather, and it did not sail until a month later.

As soon as the Armada reached the western end of the Channel it was shadowed by a

smaller English naval force under Lord Howard of Effingham. There were minor skirmishes in which the Spanish lost two ships, and a week later, on 27 July, the Armada dropped anchor off Calais and waited for Parma's army to arrive from Dunkirk. The English did not want to wait, and sent fireships into the enemy who quickly scattered. There was no opportunity of reassembling the Spanish fleet, for with worsening weather they were forced to flee northwards to return home around Scotland and western Ireland. But they were desperately short of food, water and ammunition, and roughly one-third to a half of the Armada ships and perhaps as many as two-thirds or three-quarters of the men were lost, though very few to English guns.

The discovery of Armada wrecks off Fair Isle, between the Orkney and Shetland Islands, and off western Ireland has not only filled in details of life on board several ships, but has also given some unexpected information about why the Armada failed. The wrecks of the ships *El Gran Grifon*, *Girona*, *La Trinidad Valencera* and *Santa Maria de la Rosa* contained examples of the guns and shot, and a significant proportion of this random sample was found to be either old or badly made. On the *El Gran Grifon* site were twelve guns, about one-third of the total listed for that vessel, and of these one bronze gun was found to have been poorly cast with gas voids left in the metal, and its barrel had been bored incorrectly which would have not only made it inaccurate when fired, but also weak and liable to explode when discharged. Two of the other guns were the by then obsolete, wrought-iron breech-loaders, notoriously dangerous to use and inaccurate, and there was the breech block for a third gun of that type. There were also five cast-iron guns, the more modern type that had superseded the wrought-iron and bronze guns, so the armament of the ship was not completely inadequate. Moreover, a detailed study of dozens of cast-iron shot from the Armada wrecks and an historical appraisal of how the shot was made show that they contained impurities, and, having been quenched after casting, were brittle and probably tended to shatter rather than penetrate the hull of an enemy ship. Perhaps this contributed to the Armada not succeeding in sinking any English ships.

The excavation of the *Santa Maria de la Rosa*, a large, commandeered merchant vessel of 945 tons carrying twenty-six guns and over 300 men, has revealed a small part of the bottom of the ship and shown that this Mediterranean-built vessel had a fairly weak hull not really suited to the heavy seas of the Atlantic. This too has sparked off a study of why so many Armada ships were lost in the gales that dogged their return to Spain. It is thought that since many of the large front-line ships were not built as warships, the problem may be that as comparatively weak merchantmen they were more liable to being lost.

7
Global seafaring: seventeenth to early nineteenth century

From the seventeenth to the early nineteenth century Britain was among the leading European nations who were creating trading empires around the world, but to defend and enlarge it Britain needed a Royal Navy of great size and complexity that could challenge any other sea power in the world. Since much of that story of global trade and warfare is documented in considerable detail, the role of archaeology is no longer as the major source of historical evidence. Instead it enables the objects and places mentioned in documentary sources to be illustrated and scientifically examined and so stimulates historical research into subjects that have not otherwise been studied. But documentary records are far less complete when it comes to the study of the many small ports and seafaring communities of Britain, and also of the more local European shipping, so archaeology still has a major part to play in providing basic information.

European merchantmen

The wrecks of several merchant ships engaged in European trade have been found off southern England, but generally no hull structure has remained (**65**). At Rill Cove, by the Lizard, Cornwall, a small wrought-iron breech-loading gun was found with more than 300 Spanish and Spanish-American coins of the late sixteenth to early seventeenth century. These suggest that a foreign armed merchant ship was lost there in the early seventeenth century. At Mullion Cove

nearby is the wreck of a ship that is thought to be the merchantman *Santo Christo de Castello*, wrecked in a gale in October 1667, while bound from Amsterdam to Spain on behalf of Genoese merchants. Her main cargo is documented to have included iron, lead, clothing and spices, but in the wreck have been found many iron nails and a few lead ingots. Identification is almost certain since there are various Dutch objects too, for example clay pipes from Gouda and a tobacco box lid decorated with the young Prince of Orange, as well as some Roman Catholic objects, such as a brass medallion depicting St Francis of Assisi and St Antony of Padua. Other wrecks are more difficult to date precisely, such as that off Mewstone Ledge, near Plymouth, where ten cannons have been noted with fragments of Spanish or Italian oil jars suggesting part of a cargo.

Inland and coastal vessels

A number of local vessels have also been found that reflect the transport of goods and people locally in and around Britain, and they are generally clinker built, as if many local vessels continued to be built in traditional ways dating back to the medieval period.

Several local vessels have been found in the Thames valley, the earliest being a river barge that has been carbon 14 dated probably to the early seventeenth century. It was originally about 13.7m long and perhaps 2.7m wide (45 by 9ft), and lay upside down beside the River

65 Map of seventeenth- to nineteenth-century wreck sites in Great Britain.

● = British warships;

O = foreign warships;

◆ = East Indiamen, international;

▲ = armed merchantmen.

Lea at Walthamstow in east London, and may have capsized in the old river bed. It had a thick plank-like keel suited to the shallows of the river and was built of oak with iron rivets holding the clinker planks and with trenails fastening the planks and frames. There was an inner lining or 'ceiling' of planks in the hold to protect the hull from damage by the cargo.

A somewhat similar clinker built vessel, dating from about 1670, was found sunk in the River Thames at Blackfriars, London, with a cargo of over 500 bricks probably for rebuilding London after the Great Fire of 1666 (**66, 67, 68**). Between the ribs, however, were pieces of coal, presumably traces of a former cargo of 'sea-coal' that had been brought from Newcastle to London in a collier. It seems that the vessel was a lighter used for unloading seagoing ships moored in the river so as to take the cargoes ashore. The vessel itself was 12–16m long, and 3–4m wide (39–52ft by 10–13ft), and it too had a thick plank-like keel.

Three important vessels have been found in north Wales. These are not so closely dated but reflect the important slate industry, possibly in the seventeenth century. Two were found in Lakes Padarn and Peris in north Wales, and were involved in the distribution of slate from the quarry to the coast. Both were clinker built, and the Padarn boat had sunk while carrying its cargo of about 1.85 tonnes of slates. This was a rowing vessel only 6m long and 2.16m in the beam (19.75 by 7ft), and with a flat bottom. The third was found with a cargo of some 23,000 slates sunk in the Menai Straits between the mainland and the Isle of Anglesey. It was also clinker built, the planks being held together with iron rivets, and the ribs fastened by trenails. It may have been the type of coastal vessel that collected slates from the inland craft that carried them to a seaport, perhaps Beaumaris, where they could be trans-shipped to larger vessels for distribution by sea.

Not all local vessels were clinker built in the eighteenth century, for the barge *Daresbury*, a local type known as a Mersey 'flat', has survived near Liverpool. Although built in 1772 for the Weaver Navigation Company, this remarkable carvel built survivor was still in use until 1956 and should eventually be preserved at the Boat Museum, Ellesmere Port. It is one of many recent traditional local vessels that give important clues to vessel types of long ago, their design and construction having been handed

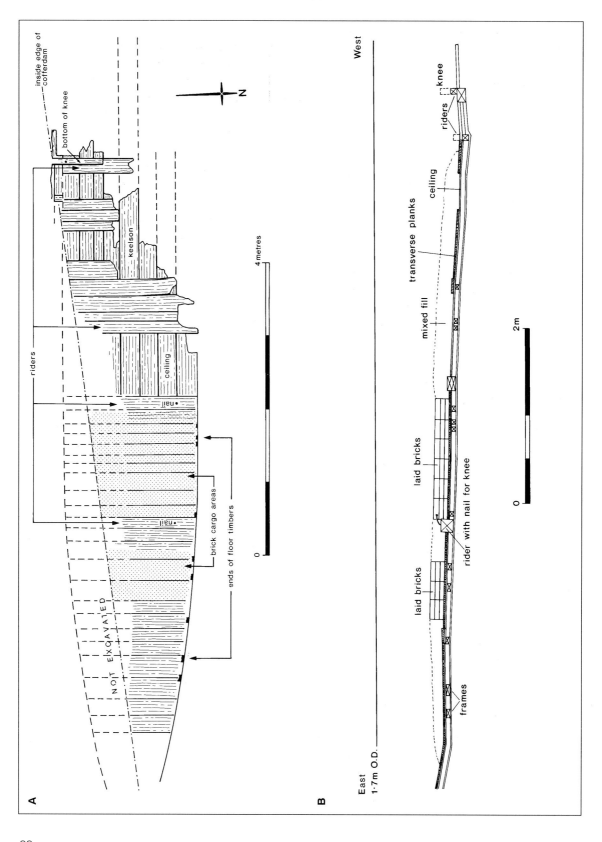

66 Blackfriars ship 2: (a) plan and (b) perspective view. (Copyright: Museum of London)

down through generations of boatbuilders. For this reason it is very important to record such craft even though many have been built relatively recently. Such a record has been made, for example, of the only remaining Norfolk Keel, a clinker built vessel of about 1800 which was sunk in 1890 to support a river bank at Whitlingham, but has since been raised. Further south, in East Sussex, the last remaining Rye barge *Primrose*, built about 1890, was raised in 1993 and is being preserved in Hastings. Although abandoned during the 1930s, this vessel is important since pictures show similar vessels at Rye dating back to about 1570 with a design and rig that had been little changed in 400 years.

Ports

By the seventeenth century the increase in the bulk trade cargoes caused existing ports in Britain to be generally overstretched. Quays were too small, cargo handling arrangements were inadequate, and by the late eighteenth century even the water depth became a problem as very large ships had to be accommodated. Although old ports often retained old facilities, important advances were made during the eighteenth century, particularly the building of enormous wet docks in some of the major ports, such as London, Liverpool and Hull. The first of these, the Howland Great Wet Dock at Rotherhithe, downstream of London, was built between 1697 and 1700 and extended over 4ha (10 acres). It was not a commercial dock at which goods were loaded and unloaded, but instead a place to lay up ships and service them in the winter months. A similar dock, but smaller, was also built at Sea Mills on the Avon around 1710, and although abandoned about 1760 parts of it still survive.

67 Diagram of Blackfriars ship 2 to show its construction. (Copyright: Museum of London)

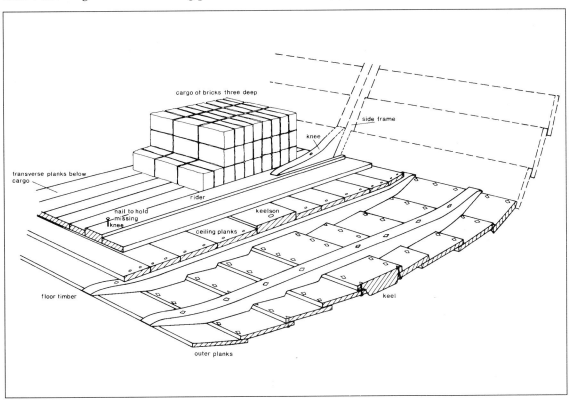

68 Ceiling planks of Blackfriars ship 2. (Photograph: Museum of London Archaeology Service. Copyright: MoL)

It was Liverpool that pioneered the earliest commercial wet dock, the Old Dock being opened in 1715. About 1.6ha (4 acres) in extent it was surrounded by warehouses and other buildings, and this new development was made possible by the port not being hedged in by the restrictive practices found at London and Bristol. It was the start of a dock building programme there that mainly extended from 1753 to 1836 and helped to make Liverpool very important and wealthy. Subsequently others were built elsewhere, such as at Hull during 1778–9. However, the technology of dock building was not always understood and could create major engineering problems. For

example, at Grimsby a new dock built in 1796 had lock walls that literally sank while the wooden floor of the lock was blown up by pressure below.

During the early nineteenth century, docks were built at many other ports, such as Leith and Edinburgh, but it was in London that there was the greatest need. Since docks gave additional quay space for cargo handling, their construction seemed to be the best way of enlarging the port whose Legal Quays, just downstream from London Bridge, for imported goods, only measured 432.5m (1419ft), though these were supplemented by 1121.6m (3680ft) of Sufference Wharves. The customs facilities were hopelessly inadequate, with ships and lighters jostling for space not only on the quayside but also for warehousing space. As late as the nineteenth century cargoes could remain piled high in ships, lighters and on the quays for weeks, and gave rise to frustrated merchants delayed in selling their goods, and to theft by gangs of organized 'lumpers' or river pirates.

The West India Company opened their dock on the Isle of Dogs in 1802, and other docks were soon built downstream. For security the West India Company enclosed their dock by a massive wall 6m (19ft) high, and a defensive ditch 1.8m deep and 3.6m wide (6 by 2ft). The design of docks was becoming more sophisticated, one of the finest, though not wholly typical, being St Katharine's Dock just downstream from the Tower of London. Built in 1828 it had two basins and an entrance basin, and is surrounded by monumental warehouses standing on iron pillars giving covered quay space below.

The study of ports during the past three centuries is a huge subject, with enormous scope for archaeological study which can only be skated over here. This is shown by the fact that in addition to the sea and river ports, there were the inland 'canal ports' that developed during the great age of canal building in the late eighteenth century, and during the nineteenth century there were also 'railway ports'.

East India trade

European trade with Asia developed mainly from about 1600 to 1800, but although East India Companies were formed in England, Netherlands, France, Denmark, Scotland, Spain, Austria and Sweden, only those of England and the Netherlands were of prime importance. The wrecks of both English and Dutch East India Company ships form a significant part of discovered maritime archaeological sites in Britain, together with a Danish East India wreck, the *Svecia*, that was lost in the Orkneys in 1740.

The basic trading pattern was to export silver and gold to Asia, and with this to purchase and return to Europe valuable spices, silks and porcelain which would then be sold at auctions. Much of the specie was purchased by the

English and Dutch companies from Spanish merchants in return for manufactured goods, the Spaniards having mined the precious metals with native labour mainly in central and south America. Silver was particularly important as it was much more valuable in Asia than in Europe, so its mere transportation to the East realized a profit. The silver was shipped in the form of ingots and coins, the latter particularly being rials-of-eight which were also known by the Spaniards as 'dollars', but in England were better known as 'pieces of eight'. In the Netherlands some of the silver was also turned into coins, such as crown-sized 'ducatons'. For over two centuries, then, large heavily armed ocean-going merchantmen known as 'East Indiamen' opened up global trade by sailing half way around the globe via the Cape, which the Dutch company first settled as a supplies base in 1652.

The English East India Company was incorporated by royal charter from Elizabeth I in 1600, when already its ships were reaching India and Japan. The Dutch East India Company, the Verenigde Oost-Indische Compagnie (usually abbreviated to VOC), was established in 1602 and immediately contested the English right to trade with the 'spice islands' between Australia and China. For many years during the first half of the seventeenth century there was virtual war between the two companies. Both companies had in effect a navy, an army, and an administration that allowed them to make treaties with Asian nations and even to wage war. The headquarters of the English company was in London, with a dockyard at Deptford downstream on the River Thames; and the Dutch company, although organized into several branches or 'chambers', had its main base in Amsterdam. The outcome of the war between the two companies, two of the largest commercial organizations that the world has ever known, was that the Dutch won the most valuable trading area of Indonesia and its 'spice islands', and built their headquarters at Batavia (nowadays Jakarta, in Java); and the

English company had to settle for second best in India, and established their primary bases at Bombay, Madras and Bengal. Eventually the Dutch company was wound up in 1798, though as a legacy of the VOC the Dutch government still retained control of Indonesia as a colony until 1949. The EIC ceased having the monopoly of trade with India in 1813 and with China in 1833, but it retained its administration of India until the company was dissolved in 1858, when the British government took over the control of India until 1947. The legacy of these two companies is therefore enormous, and their shipping losses are of great international importance as evidence of the beginnings of global trade. It is significant that on the shore of Hastings there lie the remains of the best preserved East Indiaman of any nation known in the world, two-thirds complete and still containing much of her outward bound cargo.

English East Indiamen

What the later East Indiamen were like, how they were armed, and what trade goods and supplies were carried in them is probably well represented by a number of wrecks in British waters, though very little detail about them has been published. These include the *Albion* (1765) and *Hindostan* (1803) in the Thames estuary, the *Valentine* (1779) in the Channel Islands, the *Earl of Abergavenny* (1805) off Weymouth, and the *Admiral Gardner* (1809) in the Goodwin Sands.

Sadly, the *Albion* and the *Hindostan* have only been recorded because both wrecks were plundered, the latter with a grab from the salvage ship. The result is that information about the hull construction, the cargo packaging and stowage of both ships is lost. Both vessels were outward bound for India and China with cargoes that included large quantities of silver bullion. However, among the finds from the *Albion* were 500 lead ingots, 70 of which have been recorded and had the UEIC (United East India Company) stamp. The cargo recoveries from the *Hindostan* included many small copper finger ingots as well as copper coinage of V, X and XX 'cash' pieces and some lead cloth seals with the UEIC mark. There were also many brass furniture fittings, and on the seabed were large puddles of mercury. Several medical objects were of interest: from the *Albion* were parts of a special type of early tourniquet, and from the *Hindostan* were two delftware ointment jars decorated with blue anchors and still containing their original white ointment.

The bottom of the 53.92m (177ft) long East Indiaman *Earl of Abergavenny* has survived in Weymouth Bay where she sank in 1805, and has been carefully recorded by an amateur archaeological group. This ship, built at Northfleet in 1796, was outward bound for Bengal and China under Captain John Wordsworth, brother of the poet William. The loss was due to pilot error when this heavily laden vessel was driven onto the Shambles Bank, and over 200 people perished including the captain, much to the distress of the Wordsworth family, and this was to affect William's poetry. The hull structure is massive, the outer planks being 0.127m (5in) thick, covered by an outer sheathing of softwood 22mm (1in) thick, and that too is covered by copper sheathing attached by copper nails. The planks were fastened to substantial ribs measuring 0.33 by 0.25m (1ft by 10in). Although salvaged in the past, the careful excavation of the wreck has revealed traces of the cargo and supplies, ranging from copper ingots to gun flints, medical and navigational equipment, and of course many personal possessions including gaming pieces such as a draughtsman and even a domino.

Dutch East Indiamen

Much more archaeological recording and publication has been carried out on the VOC ships sunk in British waters and these span most of the period of the company's existence. From these it has been possible to analyse parts of the cargoes, particularly the silver bullion, the life on board and the construction and armament of the vessels. In times of war in Europe these East

Indiamen were sent from the Netherlands northwards around Scotland where some were wrecked. However, the rocky seabed has meant that no hull structure has survived there. Others passed through the English Channel leaving a trail of wrecked Indiamen, though those that were wrecked on the rocky reefs of the Isles of Scilly have left little trace of hull structure.

The earliest Dutch East Indiaman wreck so far found in British waters is that of the *Campen*, sunk on the Needles, Isle of Wight, during a storm in October 1627. The vessel was of the Amsterdam 'Chamber' or branch of the company, and was outward bound for Batavia, now Jakarta, in Java. She had thirty guns and about 160 sailors, soldiers and merchants on board, and had been given instructions to avoid anchoring in English waters as the dispute between the rival Dutch and English East India Companies was then particularly serious. The Dutch had tortured and killed English East India Company sailors and merchants on the island of Amboina, and only two months before the loss of the *Campen* three Dutch ships had been detained by the English at the Isle of Wight, and their crews 'chained up'. Just why she had sailed through the Channel is not clear, but her crew was saved, as was most of the treasure. Three centuries later no hull structure remained on the seabed, though the divers, who had found the site in 1979, did discover in the rocky gullies iron shot for cannons, lead pistol and musket shot, furniture fittings, pottery, glass and pewter tableware, clay pipes, and even the bones of cattle, pig, chicken and stockfish that were once part of the ship's supplies. The ship's ballast included over 100 boat-shaped lead ingots. But the main item of discovered cargo was the treasure of about 8000 silver coins from the two remaining chests of silver that were not recovered in 1627. The coins comprised mostly leeuwendaalders of the Netherlands, though there were some Spanish-American silver 'pieces-of-eight'.

Another Dutch East Indiaman of the Amsterdam Chamber, also outward bound for Batavia, was the *Lastdrager*, which was wrecked in the Shetland Islands in March 1653, with the loss of 206 men. This ship had taken the northern route around the British Isles as England and the Netherlands were then at war. The wreck is notable for the many navigation instruments that have survived, including part of a rare Dutch mariner's universal astrolabe, no complete example of which is known to exist. There were also many dividers, portable sun-dials and a sounding lead. Part of the ship's treasure remained as over 500 silver coins, some of which were Dutch and others were Spanish-American reales. Mercury lay in puddles in rock pools on the seabed, and was presumably being exported to Asia for metal refining, for gilding, for making mirrors and for medicinal purposes, and there was evidence that it was being carried in stoneware jugs of 'Bellarmine' type. Perhaps most interesting of all were the heads of four golf clubs, among the earliest known, which were no doubt the property of someone on board. This game of Scottish origin became popular in Europe in the seventeenth and eighteenth centuries, but the wreck shows how early this popular European sport was being 'exported' to the rest of the world.

Five golf-club heads were also found in the Dutch East Indiaman *Kennermerland*, sailing to Batavia for the Amsterdam Chamber, until wrecked in December 1664 in the Shetland Islands. Its wreck debris included cannons and anchors, personal objects and items from the ship's stores and equipment, all of which was scattered widely among the rocky seabed gullies. It was discovered in 1971, and among the traces of cargo were Bellarmine stoneware flagons associated with mercury. Another Bellarmine flagon contained peach stones.

Among the later Dutch East Indiamen wrecks found in Britain are the *Princesse Maria* lost in the Scilly Isles in 1686, and the *Adelaar* sunk off the Isle of Barra in 1728, and in these no ships' structure has survived. This also applied to the outward-bound Dutch East Indiamen *De Liefde*, sunk in the Shetland Islands in 1711, and the

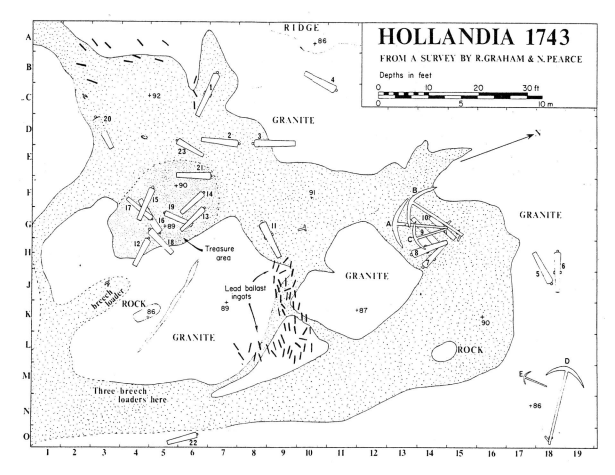

69 Plan of the scattered remains of the Dutch East Indiaman *Hollandia*, a ship similar to the *Amsterdam*, which sank in the Isles of Scilly in 1743. None of the hull structure has survived. Contrast with the intact wreck of the *Amsterdam*. (Copyright: R. Cowan)

Hollandia, lost in the Isles of Scilly in 1743. In the *De Liefde* part of a company treasure chest was found containing new minted Dutch silver ducatons. However, the *Hollandia* wreck is special in that it had never been salvaged until discovered in 1971, so the full range of silver specie for the East India trade was represented and was found as a mound nearly a metre (3ft) high (**colour plate 9**). The wreck was identified mainly by silver tableware bearing the coat of arms of the Imhoff and Bentinck families, whose members died when the ship struck Gunner Rock one night in July (**69**). A survey of the wreck debris enabled the process of the loss to

be reconstructed. The ship had sailed on for over a mile from the reef until its bottom burst open spilling out ballast and cargo, leaving the main part of the vessel to sink 60m (196ft) further on. The pattern of cannons and anchors, and the mound of more than 35,000 silver coins formerly at the stern, mean that the layout of the disappeared ship was reasonably clear. The cause of the loss was apparently poor navigation, and it is thought that Captain Jan Kelder erroneously believed that the ship was well into the Atlantic past the Scilly Isles when he turned south and struck the rock. Of particular interest, then, were the discovery of fragments of a cross-staff or back-staff, crude wooden instruments for establishing latitude, as well as parts of one of the earliest known octants, an instrument that had been invented by James Hadley as recently as 1731 for more accurately establishing latitude.

But whereas the hulls of all of these ships have decayed away, it is a twin to the *Hollandia*, the *Amsterdam*, that survives on the south coast at Hastings and is the best-preserved East Indiaman known of any nation in the world (70–73 and **colour plates 10** and **11**). This ship was on its maiden voyage for the Amsterdam Chamber and had left the Dutch coast on 8 January 1749, but on board there were some men infected with a deadly disease, for during the next two weeks 50 men died and 40 more were sick and dying. When she encountered a severe gale in Pevensey Bay and lost her rudder, the crew apparently mutinied and ran the ship ashore at high tide on 26 January. At low water those who survived the voyage walked ashore and soon after the chests of specie were saved, though personal belongings were left behind. A local guard was placed around the wreck to stop looting by local wreckers, but by the time salvage commenced the ship had sunk so deeply into the beach that salvage was impossible. In fact in three months the ship sank about 8m (26ft), and she lies there two-thirds complete and containing most of her cargo of wine, cloth and many other items originally bound for Batavia. Limited excavations have taken place and parts of the cargo of wine in onion-shaped bottles, military and medical equipment and the possessions of some of the 333 people on board have been recovered. Among them are the bones of the Captain's cabin boy, and lap dogs probably belonging to the three women passengers.

The Royal Navy

Documentary records show that during the seventeenth and eighteenth centuries there were major improvements in the design of the hull and rig of north European warships. Moreover, a characteristic feature of seventeenth-century warships was that very ornate and colourful wood carvings replaced the geometric painting of the previous century, to reflect the prestige and dignity of monarchs. During the eighteenth century such elaboration was reduced to more sensible proportions. Incidentally, it is incorrect to use the prefix HMS with a warship's name before about 1790.

During the early seventeenth century half of James I's warships were still four-masters, but by about 1640 the fourth mast had become obsolete as the size of the mizzen was increased to compensate. Later that century there were experiments with the hull construction, the *Royal James* of 1670, for example, having iron standards and knees in place of wooden ones, and about the same time some warships were sheathed in lead instead of the usual wood and tar, though this was discontinued due to corrosion of the fastenings by electrolytic action. The method of steering changed about 1700 from the inefficient mechanism called a whipstaff, a kind of enormous tiller, to be replaced by the wheel. Subsequent changes to the hull included the introduction of copper sheathing to some warships. There were initial corrosion problems from the 1760s that were solved in 1783 by the use of copper fastenings.

Archaeology is able to illustrate many of the features described above, as shown in the wreck of the warship believed to be the *Swan*, a small Cromwellian vessel lost in the Sound of Mull in 1653 while undertaking operations against the MacLeans of Duart. In it have been found examples of decorative wood carvings from the upper part of the vessel, which is most unusual as normally only the bottom of a ship survives (74). The bottom of a warship thought to be the *Matthias*, a 54-gun prize that blew up during a Dutch attack on the English fleet anchored in the River Medway in 1667, may be typical. The hull bottom was found during excavations for a new dock basin at Chatham Dockyard in 1876 on land that had been reclaimed from the river, and a plan of the remains shows that the surviving hull was 28m long and 9.75m wide (92 by 32ft), though one end, thought to be the stern, had been destroyed. Around the wreck were fourteen iron cannons, 6-, 9- and 24-pounders, scattered as if reflecting the final

70 *(Opposite)* Dutch East India Company guns from the *Amsterdam*, cast 1748.

71 Plan of the *Amsterdam* as she lies in the beach at Hastings and (right) a reconstructed side elevation. She was beached in 1749 and quickly sank deep into the seabed.

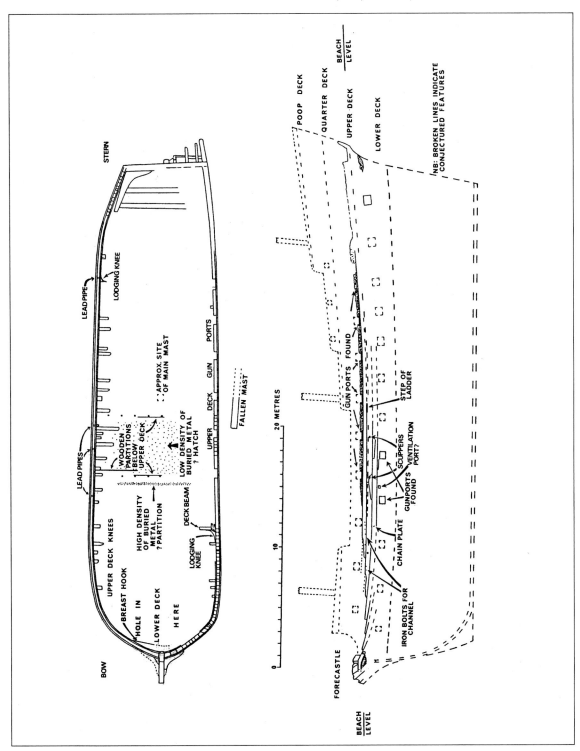

72 Bow of the *Amsterdam*.

73 Reconstruction of the *Amsterdam*.

74 Carved decorative timber from a wreck believed to be that of the warship *Swan*, lost off Mull in 1653. It shows the harp symbol of Ireland. Overall length of the piece is 550mm. (Reproduced by kind permission of Colin Martin)

explosion of the ship. The oak hull was particularly interesting for it had been heavily strengthened by large timber knees that held cross timbers known as the 'St Andrew's Cross' to strengthen the hold.

In 1660, during the interval between the First and Second Dutch Wars, the city of Amsterdam presented Charles II on his 'restoration' with the *Mary*, the first English royal yacht. It was a vessel of 100 tonnes armed with eight guns, but was not successful outside Dutch waters. Consequently in 1661 it was transferred to English naval use as a transport vessel for notables, and it was during one such voyage, between Dublin and Chester, in 1675 that it was wrecked off Anglesey. Thirty-five men, including the Captain and the Earl of Meath, were lost. The wreck was found in 1971, and in it were nine bronze guns, one of them Dutch bearing the date 1660.

A scatter of cannons on the seabed at the base of Tearing Ledge, near Bishop Rock in the Isles of Scilly, is an important clue to the identity of another vessel. At first it was thought to be the warship *Romney*, a 50-gun, fifth rate vessel which was part of the fleet commanded by Admiral Sir Cloudisley Shovell that struck the Western Rocks in October 1707. But the *Romney*'s largest guns were 12-pounders and the largest of those on the site were apparently 32-pounders. Moreover, sixty-two guns were found, so it is more likely to be the larger ship of that fleet, the *Eagle*, which carried up to seventy guns. However, its largest were still 24-pounders, which does not explain the existence

of five 32-pounder guns on the site. Perhaps they were being used as ballast.

No part of the wooden hull of the Tearing Ledge ship has survived, but its construction was probably originally similar to that of two English warships lost in 1690. One of these is the 70-gun ship *Anne*, beached and burnt at Pett Level near Rye, East Sussex, in July that year to stop her being taken as a French prize. The vessel had been seriously damaged in the Battle of Beachy Head against the French navy which was then supporting exiled James II's abortive attempt to reclaim his English throne. The entire hull bottom survives since she had sunk deep into the soft seabed and may be seen when the tides are particularly low (**75** and front cover). The *Anne* is the only surviving substantially unaltered part of a warship of the Restoration navy of Charles II and is one of his 'thirty ships', which have been called one of the most important in the history of the British Navy, for they set a large number of precedents for the design and construction of future warships, and in particular they were some of the first ships planned from their inception as line-of-battle ships. Moreover, the *Anne* has very close connections with Samuel Pepys, Secretary to the Admiralty, and having seen exceptional royal service under James II as well as under William

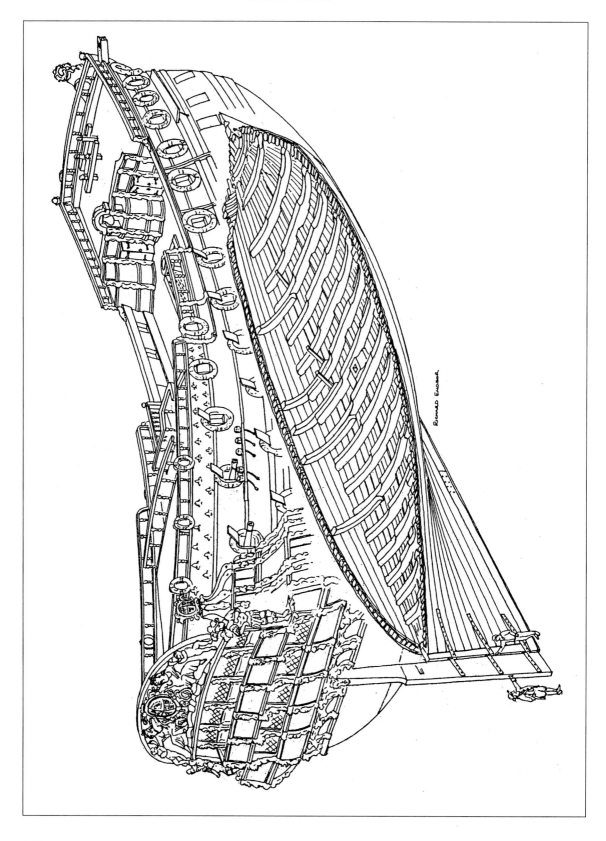

75 Reconstruction by Richard Endsor of the remains of the 70-gun warship *Anne,* sunk in the beach between Hastings and Rye in 1690. The upper part of the hull was burnt away to save her from being taken as a French prize. (Copyright: Richard Endsor)

and Mary she is considered worthy of preservation – particularly as a valuable link between the *Mary Rose* (1545) and HMS *Victory* (*c*. 1800).

In contrast only part of the bottom of the small frigate *Dartmouth* survives. This fifth rate, lost in a violent storm off Mull, western Scotland, in October 1690, was excavated in 1973 when part of its elm keel was found together with adjacent carvel planking of elm, and the lower parts of oak frames fastened together by trenails. Outboard there was a sheathing of fir, and between this and the main planking was a layer of hair and tar to protect the hull from marine borers like the 'shipworm' *Teredo*. The *Dartmouth* is almost the only English warship wreck to have been studied and published in detail, and in it were not only loose fittings, such as lead scupper pipes, from higher up in the hull, but also nineteen of her guns, three anchors and even the ship's bronze bell dated 1678. A mass of other items was recovered ranging from wooden pulley blocks from the rigging, to bricks and tiles probably from the galley. Table utensils such as wine bottles, a pewter plate and a brass spoon have been found, as well as a remarkable variety of clay pipes. Other objects, particularly navigational and surgical instruments, await publication.

The *Anne* and *Dartmouth* are part of an important group of discovered warship wrecks which if studied collectively should tell us much about the construction and equipage of naval ships. They include the *Coronation* lost off Penlee Point, Plymouth, in 1691, the *Sapphire*, sunk off New Foundland in 1696, and the *Restoration* and *Newfoundland* sunk into the Goodwin Sands, off eastern Kent, in the Great Gale of 1703. But apart from the *Sapphire*, little has been published about these sites.

A particularly interesting wreck, however, has been identified as the 70-gun, third rate warship *Stirling Castle*, which was swallowed by the Goodwin Sands in the Great Gale of 1703 with the loss of 206 men. Most of its hull below its gundeck was found to be intact when it was examined by divers in 1979. The sands had moved and exposed one side of the vessel so that it was possible to see gunports, with one apparently still having a gun in position. The ship's bell had the naval broad arrow and the date 1701. In the short time before the wreck began to collapse and the sands closed around again divers managed to recover many objects, including two large copper kettles from the galley, and parts of muskets and swivel guns. A particularly fascinating discovery was a sea-chest crushed beneath a gun, and in it a wooden navigational cross-staff, a Gunter scale, a pocket microscope, nine pairs of dividers, and a set of five sizes of sand glasses. Other finds included onion-shaped wine bottles, a wooden bowl, a belaying pin, pulley blocks, a folding seat or table, a floor brush and a scrubbing brush. A fine collection of pewter tableware was found in the galley area, and elsewhere various personal objects such as shoes, a toothbrush and a comb.

Dating from only three years later is another warship wreck containing many well-preserved objects. This is the *Hazardous*, a third rate French ship with fifty guns, built in 1698, which had been captured by the English in 1703. In November 1706 she ran aground in Bracklesham Bay during a gale while escorting a fleet of merchantmen up the Channel from Dartmouth to the Downs off Kent. The wreck was found in 1977, with the collapsed port side having survived under wreck debris. Traces of a deck remained together with a line of cannons as if they had fallen from a gun deck, and with one of them was a considerable part of a wooden carriage. Many of the usual personal objects and parts of the ship's equipment were found, such as pulley blocks, navigation instruments, pewter tableware and shoe buckles. But of particular interest is the caulking between the ship's outer planking for this was held in place by lead strips.

Other warship wrecks, reported as having been found in British waters, are the *Association* (Scilly Isles, 1707), *Firebrand* (Scilly Isles, 1707), *Assurance* (Isle of Wight, 1753), *Ramillies* (Devon, 1760), *Juno* (Scilly Isles, 1782), *Halsewell* (Devon, 1786), *Weazle* (Devon, 1799), *Impregnable* (Hampshire, 1799) and *Pomone* (Isle of Wight, 1811), but these have not been archaeologically published.

Two warship wrecks of the later eighteenth century are of particular interest, the first being the *Invincible*, sunk in the Solent after grounding on a sandbank in February 1758. She was part of a fleet bound for Halifax, Newfoundland, and was fully stocked with supplies. A study of the site suggests that the hull of the ship, a 74-gun third rate that had been captured from the French in 1747, lies in great slabs on the seabed, and around it are objects that are exceptionally well preserved. These include equipment from the stores of the boatswain, gunners and carpenters, such as pulley blocks, many leather buckets, brushes, grenades and lead musket shot. Many wooden utensils for use by the crew were found, including spoons, bowls, a stave tankard and square plates. There were of course parts of clothing, including shoes, some of which were, surprisingly, for women and children. A few shoes were marked 'DC', meaning 'Dead men's Cloathes', which had previously been sold on behalf of the widows of dead sailors. There were also many buttons, some regimental and others naval, the latter using the naval 'fouled anchor', a rope twisted around the anchor, at a time that is rather earlier than had been supposed. The ship has provided some interesting surprises, such as that the false keel was found to have been coppered at a date which is earlier than official written records show that even partial coppering was occurring.

The other wreck lies in the Isles of Scilly, and here too the finds also include evidence of experimental design, in this case in the central

brass bush of pulley wheels. The wreck is the *Colossus*, a 74-gun third rate, which sank on a reef near the island of Sampson in December 1798 while returning from the Mediterranean. On board she had about 200 Greek vases in eight crates, part of the collection of Sir William Hamilton, but when the wreck was found in 1974 these vases were found smashed into 35,000 fragments scattered over the seabed. They were carefully collected and parts of some vases have been restored by the British Museum.

Naval dockyards

There is insufficient space here to discuss the surviving buildings and former activities of the royal dockyards, but it would be wrong to pass them by since they serviced the Navy. The modern closure of historic dockyards means that the opportunity of preserving important and typical historic naval buildings has become a serious option. Portsmouth was the first royal dockyard, having been established about 1496, and it was soon followed by dockyards at Woolwich (1512) and Deptford (1513). The need for further naval dockyards increased during the latter half of the seventeenth century with Harwich (1652), Sheerness (1665) and Plymouth (1691) being created, and abroad Port Royal, Jamaica, was established about 1675. Expanding British naval activities led to more overseas dockyards in the eighteenth century, at Gibraltar and at Port Mahon, Minorca, and there was much naval use of the ports of English Harbour in Antigua, at Halifax in Nova Scotia, and in Barbados. The pressure of the war against Napoleon led to further dockyard facilities being created in Malta (1800) and at Pembroke (1815).

Some dockyards could also provide important information about early warships that were reused as breakwaters and foundations. For example the *Lennox*, a third rate built in 1678, became a breakwater at Sheerness in 1756; the *Medway Prize*, a fourth rate captured in 1697, was sunk as a foundation at Sheerness in 1712; and the *Poole*, a fifth rate of 1696, became a foundation at Harwich in 1737. None of these has yet been found.

Foreign naval ships

It is not surprising to find that a number of foreign warships were wrecked while passing the British Isles, particularly north of Scotland in times of war. The earliest so far found is possibly a Danish warship named *Wrangels Palais* which ran aground in thick fog on the Shetland Islands in 1687, while pursuing Barbary pirates. Two bronze guns have so far been recovered. Another was a Dutch warship, the *Curacao*, which was also wrecked on the Shetland Islands in 1729 while convoying a fleet of returning East Indiamen. The wreck was represented by concentrations of objects in three deep narrow gullies in the rocky seabed. There was little value in the distribution of the objects, though the two wrought-iron anchors are unlikely to have been moved much by the sea. The ship, originally 44.2m (145ft) long and under the command of Captain Jan Raije, carried forty-four guns, parts of which were found broken into more than thirty pieces. There were also five small breech-

loading swivel guns bearing the crossed anchors mark of the Admiralty of Amsterdam. Small arms were represented by fragments of muskets and pistols with their lead shot, and domestic life on board was represented by sherds of stoneware jugs, cooking pots, porcelain plates, and by glass wine and gin bottles, as well as forks, spoons and knives. Among a mixture of other small objects were, remarkably, small fragments of the pages of a printed book.

Another warship wreck found in the Shetland Islands was the armed transport ship *Evstafii* of the Imperial Russian Navy. Originally 39.62m long and 9.44m wide (130 by 31ft), it carried thirty-six guns when it was wrecked in a gale on 17 September 1780, while on a voyage apparently from Archangel, around North Cape, to Kronstadt near St Petersburg in the Gulf of Finland. Although the hull had been completely smashed there were in the rock gullies of the site parts of eighteen cast-iron guns whose poor quality reflected the contemporary

76 The Whitstable wreck, about 1700, from which objects have been recovered but not recorded.

view in the seventeenth and eighteenth centuries that Russian guns generally were 'not very good and are sold at very low prices'. About 220 Russian and Dutch coins helped to identify the wreck, and included gold roubles of Catherine II minted at St Petersburg in 1767 and 1768, and silver rouble pieces dated as late as 1776. The latest coin, however, was a Dutch silver rijksdaalder of 1779 and was presumably acquired by the Russians through the extensive Dutch trade in the Baltic. There were many parts of the ship's equipment, particularly various types of shot, and a variety of personal possessions including a silver medal commemorating the Russian victory over the Turks at the naval battle of Tchesme, opposite the Greek island of Chios, in June 1770.

Although many discoveries have been referred to in this chapter, and some of the wreck sites are protected by the government as historic monuments of national importance, it is necessary to say that comparatively little archaeological detail has yet been published (76). Sadly, most published information about sites and finds, much of which has been in government ownership, is only to be found in saleroom auction catalogues or in popular diving magazines. Meanwhile, the salvage and recovery of antiquities from underwater sites continues to occur, so the most urgent need is to rescue as much information as possible through a national programme of archaeological publication. It is only then that the true historical value of the sites can be evaluated.

8
From sail to steam and beyond

The period after about 1820 saw immense changes in ship design, construction and propulsion, in armament, in ports and cargo handling methods, and in the patterns of trade and warfare. There is only space here for the briefest outline and that cannot do justice to the enormity of the changes which, because they occurred relatively recently, have left much surviving evidence.

The change in building ships from wood to iron and then to steel was brought about by many factors, such as the lack of available cheap timber for wooden shipbuilding. But it was the industrial revolution in Britain which established the economic means of producing iron and brought into being the steam engine which transformed ship technology. The first stirrings of the changes occurred in the eighteenth century as experimenters such as Matthew Boulton and James Watt developed new methods of power and iron production. Thereafter the story becomes complex, and very interesting.

Effective steam power in ships had begun to be developed during the 1780s in France, America and Britain, one of the earliest experimental vessels being the *Charlotte Dundas*, a wooden steam tug-boat with a paddle-wheel whose engine was built on behalf of Lord Dundas by William Symington in 1801 for use on the Forth and Clyde canal. This internationally important vessel, built at Grangemouth Dockyard, has been described as

the 'first practical steamboat', for in 1802 she successfully towed two loaded vessels on the canal for 31.4km (19.5 miles) in six hours. She was 17m long, 5.5m wide and 2.4m deep (55.75 by 18 by 8ft), but as the wash from the steam tug threatened to damage the canal banks it was decided to abandon the *Charlotte Dundas* in a creek of the canal until broken up in 1861. A photograph of her remains taken in 1856 exists to show exactly where she lay at Bainsford, just north of Falkirk, and it is just possible that a search may reveal her bottom and collapsed parts of her sides to show exactly how she was constructed.

In 1803 the American engineer Robert Fulton demonstrated a small steam-powered boat on the River Seine in Paris, and by 1807 he was running a paddle steamer service on the Hudson River. Five years later the *Comet*, which sailed on the Clyde between Greenock and Glasgow, was the first merchant steamship in Europe, and she was followed in 1816 by the first crossing of the English Channel by a paddle steamer. The development of steam power was by now rapid, and in 1838 Isambard Kingdom Brunel established the first reliable trans-Atlantic paddle steamer service with his *Great Western*, but she was a wooden ship. Brunel, however, became convinced that the screw propeller was much better than paddles and that an iron hull was preferable to a wooden hull. He introduced both of these in his steamship *Great Britain*, launched at Bristol in 1843, and now restored there after having been rescued from the Falkland Islands in 1970 (**77, 78**). This, the first propeller-driven vessel to cross the Atlantic, was 98m (321ft) long, but even this was dwarfed by its successor the *Great Eastern*, a propeller and screw-driven ship 210m (689ft) long. Although both were steam driven, each had six masts and a very large sail area because of the somewhat limited use of steam power for very long voyages. These ships were ahead of their time, but they did show the way ahead for the future of shipping.

The British navy was slow to use iron and steel, though by the early nineteenth century the use of wrought-iron fittings replacing certain timbers in wooden ships had already been adopted. Wrought-iron brackets, for example, were used to reinforce the wooden knees in HMS *Victory*, the 104-gun first rate warship now reconstructed and preserved at Portsmouth (**79, 80**). Those knees held deck beams to the sides of the hull and are thought to have been in place by 1805, though it should be mentioned that the ship has been so extensively restored that very little of its present structure has been afloat, let alone took part in the Battle of Trafalgar. This early stage in the change from wood to an iron hull is also represented in the 1805 wreck of the East Indiaman *Earl of Abergavenny*, off Weymouth, where iron knees have been found on the seabed.

77 *Great Britain* restored at Bristol.

S.S. GREAT BRITAIN

78 *Great Britain:* the iron hull before restoration.

79 HMS *Victory* as restored at Portsmouth. (Photograph: R. F. W. Cramp. Copyright: Barnaby's Picture Library)

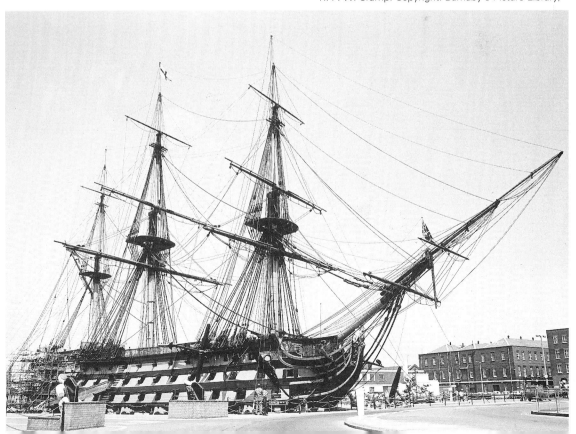

80 HMS *Victory* reconstruction showing a substantial amount of replaced old structure.

Iron strengthening plates also helped support the hanging knees in the still surviving warship HMS *Trincomalee*, a 46-gun wooden sailing frigate built in the East India Company's dockyard in Bombay during 1817, and long afloat at Portsmouth because she was constructed from Malabar Teak (**81**). She is now preserved at Hartlepool. Another sailing frigate, HMS *Unicorn*, built at Chatham and launched in 1824, is preserved at Victoria Dock, Dundee, but having been built during a time of peace she was roofed over immediately without masts, and is now a popular attraction for visitors. Here there are more extensive iron fittings, including wrought-iron knees and, at the bow, great iron 'breast hooks' that reinforce the hull.

Although the first iron steamship had already been built by 1824 and was used on the Seine, the Royal Navy was still reluctant to adopt steam power and the iron hull as late as 1842, when the Admiralty refused the offer of an iron warship that an enterprising shipbuilder had constructed. But not long after this the French navy invested in building with iron and in 1859 they completed the first of three new warships whose wooden hull was armoured with massive wrought-iron plates – the first 'ironclad'. A response to this threat to Britain's naval supremacy had to be made and a British warship with an entirely iron hull, the *Warrior*, was built and launched in 1860 (**82**). Now restored and preserved at Portsmouth, this remarkable vessel, 115m (377ft) long, also included a further development, a steam engine, though she also carried sails set on three masts.

The early steamships were not as successful as they might have been for their steam engines worked on only one cylinder, and it was not until the two-cylinder compound engine was introduced in 1865 that the problem was tackled. This was brought about by the much cheaper manufacture of iron and by better made boilers able to withstand the considerable pressure. But even this was not enough to place the steamship entirely ahead of sail since the engine and the fuel occupied so much of the space amidships which should otherwise be for the cargo. Even the opening of the Suez Canal in 1869, thereby cutting off 8000km (5000 miles) from the sailing route around the Cape, was not enough to enable steamships to compete, for fast sailing vessels had a higher cargo capacity and offered proportionally lower freight charges than did steam-driven ships.

Consequently the clipper *Cutty Sark*, preserved at Greenwich, and launched at Dumbarton in 1869 to carry tea from China, was a successful fast ship (83). Moreover, she

demonstrates just how slow was the general change from wood to iron for her construction was composite – an elm keel, iron frames and teak planking. Although the *Cutty Sark* is the only complete British clipper, archaeology is giving the remains of others. On the shore near Beachy Head, for example, lies the bottom of the wool clipper *Coonatto*, built in London in 1863, but wrecked in 1876 on a voyage from Adelaide. Here at low tide the hull of the ship can be studied, with its diagonal wooden planking fastened to iron ribs. An important factor about wrecks such as this is that

81 HMS *Trincomalee* at Portsmouth before her restoration.

82 HMS *Warrior* as restored at Portsmouth.

83 *(Opposite) Cutty Sark* as restored at Greenwich. (Photograph: Philip Beasley. Copyright: Barnaby's Picture Library)

constructional features must date from before the loss, whereas the construction of surviving historic ships may not all date from the original construction, and the age of any modifications is not always clear.

The clippers were exceptional, however, for the bulk of nineteenth-century trading vessels were ordinary, plodding, wooden sailing ships whose wrecks litter the seabed around the world. Each has a tragic story, and just one, lying in the seabed about 11.2km (7 miles) off Hastings, may be typical. It was a Danish wooden sailing ship, judging from the Copenhagen manufacturer's name on the ship's iron stove and pump, and it sank about 1861, probably in a collision. The lower part of the wooden hull is still filled with the cargo that includes hundreds of corked bottles of Cognac each with a lead cap stamped 'VIEUX COGNAC', and some bottles even have slight traces of the printed paper labels. There were small bottles of French cosmetics, many Dutch gin bottles, and many cases of then old flintlock muskets. Also there was a tombstone for the grave of a woman and her new-born baby destined for the cemetery at St Thomas in the then Danish (now American) Virgin Islands. Mother and child had died in 1858 and, curiously, the inscription was carved in English. The identity of the ship is uncertain, but it is possible that she was carrying supplies to the Confederates in the American Civil War. This is perhaps one of the many ships of the past that had set sail perhaps never to be heard of again, though archaeology underwater around Britain has the ability of completing their story.

The technical developments needed for the final change from sail to steam did not occur until the 1880s, though even then sailing merchant ships continued to be used well into the twentieth century. These developments were the cheap availability of steel, a much stronger material replacing iron, which enabled the much higher pressure triple-cylinder boilers on steam engines to be constructed. Consequently, in 1881 the steamship *Aberdeen* was able to sail

from Plymouth to Melbourne, Australia, in only forty-two days with 4000 tonnes of cargo and only one coaling stop. Cheap to build, reliable to use, and at last having a competitive cargo capacity meant that steamships could now replace the sailing merchant ship. Nowadays the wrecks of many nineteenth-century steamships on the seabed around Britain give us the opportunity of examining and illustrating the earliest methods of iron ship construction and propulsion.

The development of warships during the latter half of the nineteenth century was equally fundamental, though it was not until the last thirty years of the century that warships first gained central batteries of much larger guns, and masts and sails were finally abandoned to give types of warship that are more recognizable as 'modern'. This is the importance of the graveyard of warships of the German Grand Fleet at Scapa Flow in the Orkney Islands. Here the fleet had been interned following the Armistice in 1918, but on 21 June 1919, the German Rear-Admiral von Reuter secretly ordered the fleet to be scuttled, and 52 out of 74 vessels sank completely. Most were subsequently salvaged, but to this day there are three battleships, four cruisers and four destroyers on the bottom, giving a fascinating view of naval shipping in World War I.

There is a final type of warship that was to become very important, the submarine. As early as the sixteenth century men had played around with ideas for an underwater warship, but it was only with the use of iron in ship construction in the nineteenth century that it was realized by a few enthusiasts that a submarine could at last be built. John Holland, an Irishman who had settled in the United States in 1873, is the father of the submarine, for he built the first practical vessels. His initial submarine, lozenge-shaped and only 4.4m (14.5ft) long, was built in New York but sank in the Passaic River at Paterson, New Jersey, in 1878. It is preserved in the fine museum there. He went on to develop better submarines, and it

was to his design that in 1901 Britain's first submarine was built – a cigar-shaped vessel 19.25m (63ft) long. After twelve years of service she sank off Plymouth in 1913 while being towed to shipbreakers. Known as *Holland I* because she was the Royal Navy's first submarine, she was found and raised in 1982 and is preserved at the Submarine Museum, Gosport (**84**). This ancestor of the modern nuclear submarine is the earliest of the many submarine vessels known to lie on the seabed around Britain. They are found from time to time, such as in 1973 when the German submarine *U48* briefly emerged from the Goodwin Sands where she had been attacked in November 1917, only to sink back soon afterwards.

Lifeboats are another specialized type of vessel of enormous importance, particularly as Britain was the first nation in the world to

84 HM Submarine Torpedo Boat 'No. 1' (aka *Holland I*) (Holland-class) under way with seven crew on deck in full uniform. This submarine has been raised from the seabed and is being preserved. (Reproduced by permission of the Royal Navy Submarine Museum)

establish, in 1824, a comprehensive organization to save life at sea, the Royal National Lifeboat Institution. The first maintained lifeboats were private ventures, the earliest recorded being in use at Formby, Lancashire in 1777. The earliest surviving is the *Zetland*, built in 1800 and now preserved at Redcar, Cleveland. The first lifeboats were rowing and sailing vessels whose qualities needed to be exceptional. Lifeboats should be unsinkable, self-righting, able to be launched and beached safely as well as be propelled without difficulty. It is amazing that lifeboats that addressed these and other ideals did not

85 *Lizzie Porter* is typical of the many pulling and sailing lifeboats which formed the bulk of the RNLI fleet in the late nineteenth and early twentieth centuries. She is preserved at the National Lifeboat Museum, Chatham Historic Dockyard. (Reproduced by permission of the RNLI)

begin to exist until 1785 when Lionel Lukin converted a Norwegian yawl, and subsequently designed an 'unimmergible' coble that saved many lives off Yorkshire. But it was not until 1891 that there was developed the first powered lifeboat, *The Duke of Northumberland*, which was propelled by a kind of waterjet, but this method was soon replaced by a screw propeller. The earliest powered lifeboats burned oil and had steam

engines, but the first petrol engine vessel was built at Folkestone in 1904. The superiority of motor-powered boats was assured, though they only slowly replaced the pulling and sailing lifeboats whose last example was withdrawn from service at Whitby as recently as 1957. Typical of the many early pulling and sailing lifeboats that formed the bulk of the RNLI's fleet in the late nineteenth and early twentieth centuries is the *Lizzie Porter*, built in 1909 and serving until 1936 on the Northumbrian coast during which time she saved seventy-seven lives (85). A feature of these early lifeboats are the fore and aft 'end boxes' or watertight compartments that provided buoyancy for self-righting. The *Lizzie Porter* is preserved with later examples of lifeboats in the Royal

National Lifeboat Collection on exhibition in Chatham Historic Dockyard.

The twentieth-century development of ships and ports is beyond the bounds of this book's space, though they are no less historically important. Hovercraft and nuclear-powered vessels are among the latest developments in ship design and propulsion, and the packaging of cargoes into containers has transformed the layout of ports. Indeed, being surrounded by such a wealth of surviving ships, boats, ports and other buildings means that instead of preserving the chance discoveries of the distant past we are able to choose typical or important examples. In many ways the best means of preservation is by protecting some recent ships as historic monuments so that they are not unnecessarily damaged or destroyed, rather as typical or outstanding recent buildings are protected by 'listing'. Much thought needs to be given to what should be protected, such as, say, a sunken typical oil tanker, or the piece of a Mulberry Harbour from 1944 which lies on the seabed off Pagham. Both represent circumstances of global historical importance, and both show that monuments to Britain's maritime past will continue to accumulate as future centuries roll by. Britain will always be an island nation, despite the Channel Tunnel, whose shipping and ports will remain essential to its survival, so an understanding of the history of the ships and seafarers using its ports and passing through its territorial waters is fundamental to appreciating a wider view of its history in Europe and in the world.

Glossary

Although nautical dictionaries show variations in the meaning of nautical words, the following used in this book have these meanings:

bilge The lowest part of the interior of a ship.

boat A small vessel usually used in inland waters.

bulkhead An internal cross-partition or wall in a ship.

carvel Edge-to-edge planking to give a smooth-sided hull.

caulking The wadding lying in the seam between planks or in scarf joints and repairs, to make the hull watertight.

ceiling The planks lining the interior of a vessel inside the ribs.

clinker Overlapping outboard planking of a boat's hull.

hull The main body of a ship or boat.

port side The left-hand side of a ship looking forward.

shell-built A vessel that has been built with planks first, to which the ribs have been added as a strengthening. Shell-building is only possible when there is a system of fastening planks to each other, as in Scandinavian clinker built vessels using rivets, or in classical ships of the Mediterranean using mortice-and-tenon joints.

ship A large vessel able to sail on voyages for considerable periods of time.

side rudder A rudder hung on the side of a ship near the stern.

skeleton-built A vessel built first with a skeleton framework of keel, ribs and endposts, to which a skin of planks has been added subsequently.

starboard side The right-hand side of a ship looking forward.

steering oar A long oar used for steering, fastened over the stern of a vessel. Particularly used in inland waters. Not to be confused with a side rudder.

strake A line of planks of the outer skin of a ship.

trenail A wooden nail used to fasten timbers together, normally more than 10mm in diameter. Those smaller than that are termed 'pegs'.

yard A horizontal spar located on a mast from which a sail is set.

Places to visit

In suggesting museums and places to visit where important objects or vessels from British maritime sites are on exhibition, it is necessary to limit these to public museums since they have a permanent responsibility for the objects that are held, and private museums are more likely to close. However, there are a number of important private collections of artefacts from seventeenth-century and later shipwrecks in British waters which are currently on public display at Penzance, Charlestown, Bembridge (Isle of Wight) and Great Yarmouth. Exhibitions at museums are always changing, and if a visit is being planned it is well worth checking with the museum that the items of interest are able to be seen.

Although a number of prehistoric plank-built vessels have been found in Britain and are being preserved, none is yet on public exhibition. These include the Brigg boat and small fragments of the North Ferriby boats which are at the National Maritime Museum, Greenwich, and the Dover boat which is being studied in Dover. However, a few of the many Bronze Age tools and weapons from the Langdon Bay 'wreck' at Dover are exhibited at the British Museum. The Hasholme dugout canoe is being preserved for exhibition at the Hull and East Riding Museum, Hull.

Fragments of the Roman ships from Blackfriars and County Hall in London are on exhibition at the Shipwreck Heritage Centre, Hastings, and at the Tower Pageant, on Tower Hill, London. The extremely well-preserved Roman lighthouse can be visited in Dover Castle, and in the nearby Dover Museum are objects from the Roman naval base of the *Classis Britannica*. The timbers of the Roman vessels from St Peter Port, Guernsey, and Magor, Gwent, are being preserved and are expected to be on exhibition in nearby localities in due course.

Although several Saxon and medieval craft have been found there is again little on exhibition. The Graveney boat, stored at the National Maritime Museum, Greenwich, is awaiting final preservation, though a cast of its remains is on exhibition, as is a useful cast of part of the impression of the Sutton Hoo ship. The treasures from the Sutton Hoo burial are exhibited at the British Museum and include information about that ship. Fragments of the fifteenth-century Blackfriars barge, from London, are to be seen at the Shipwreck Heritage Centre, Hastings, together with two large medieval ship rudders from Rye Bay. Also, several small pieces of medieval vessels from London are exhibited in the Tower Pageant, on Tower Hill, London. A group of fifteenth-century ship timbers from a medieval boatyard at Poole are to be seen in the Waterfront Museum on Poole Quay, Poole. The important early fourteenth-century lanterned lighthouse known as St Catherine's Oratory near Niton and Chale on the Isle of Wight is well worth a visit. To gain an impression of what a medieval port was like a visit to King's Lynn in Norfolk would be of value since there are the medieval houses of rich merchants close to the present waterfront. Although the medieval waterfront cannot be seen, the modern quayside does not seem to be too far removed from the scene long ago, and the mudflats exposed at low tide undoubtedly hold a great store of archaeological evidence about the medieval port.

The special exhibit of the sixteenth century which should not be missed is the *Mary Rose* Ship Hall and Museum at Portsmouth, where the ship itself is being preserved together with the wonderful collection of objects recovered from inside. Apart from that a small selection of objects from the Spanish Armada wreck of the *Girona* is to be seen at the Ulster Museum in Belfast. At the Waterfront Museum at Poole there is part of the hull and other objects from the Studland Bay wreck, an armed sixteenth-century merchant vessel.

The Maritime Museum, Ramsgate, possesses an excellent collection of objects from warship wrecks, particularly the *Stirling Castle*, lost in the Goodwin Sands during the Great Gale of 1703; and in the museum at St Mary's, Isles of Scilly, are objects from local eighteenth- and nineteenth-century wrecks, including the warships lost in the naval disaster of 1707 when the fleet of Admiral Sir Cloudisley Shovell ran onto the rocks. Objects from this fleet are also to be seen at the Shipwreck Heritage Centre, Hastings, together with items from the warship *Anne*, sunk in the beach near Rye in 1690. The wreck of the *Anne* can be seen at exceptionally low tides off Pett Level, between Hastings and Rye, where there is a public notice on the shore outlining her story. A permanent exhibition of the archaeological work on an English warship lost locally in 1653 is to be seen in Duart Castle, Mull.

The Dutch East India Company wrecks of the seventeenth and eighteenth centuries in British waters are featured in the Shetland County Museum, Lerwick, which possesses a remarkable collection from several Indiamen;

and objects from the *Amsterdam* (1749) are featured at the Shipwreck Heritage Centre, Hastings. The wreck of the *Amsterdam* can be seen at the low monthly spring tides in the beach at Bulverhythe, between Hastings and Bexhill. Many objects from Dutch East Indiamen wrecked around Britain are also to be found in the Rijksmuseum and in the Scheepvaartmuseum in Amsterdam.

From the nineteenth and twentieth centuries there are extremely important collections at the National Maritime Museum, Greenwich, and at the Merseyside Maritime Museum, Liverpool. There are also important collections in many local port museums around the country, such as at the Maritime Museum for East Anglia, Great Yarmouth, and in the Maritime Museum at Buckler's Hard, Beaulieu.

Britain is extremely rich in surviving historic ships and in recent years major efforts have been made to save, preserve and restore them. HMS *Victory* is, of course, the best known since she was Admiral Nelson's flagship, though she has been so extensively rebuilt several times since her original construction in 1765 that hardly any of what can be seen at Portsmouth Historic Dockyard ever took part in the Battle of Trafalgar in 1805, let alone has been to sea. So, from a strictly archaeological point of view she is essentially a replica of the vessel that took part in that famous battle. However, from a naval point of view it is normal for ships to have repairs and rebuilds, and they become part of the same vessel, rather as an historic house has many additions and alterations. While in the Dockyard it is also of value to see the Royal Naval Museum.

HMS *Trincomalee*, built in 1817, is an entirely different matter, however, for comparatively little restoration of this wooden sailing warship has been necessary because she was built of teak. She is now on public exhibition at Jackson Dock, Hartlepool. Equally well preserved is the wooden sailing frigate HMS *Unicorn*, built in 1824, and preserved afloat at Victoria Dock, Dundee. At Portsmouth is preserved the beautifully restored warship HMS *Warrior*, built in 1859 and considered to be 'the first modern warship' for she has an iron hull and was powered by a steam engine and screw propeller as well as by sail. HMS *Gannet*, built in 1878, is a somewhat similar transitional warship incorporating steam and sail power, though it has a timber hull and iron frames, and can be seen at Chatham Historic Dockyard.

Two nineteenth-century merchant ships are especially noteworthy. The iron steamer SS *Great Britain*, built by Isambard Brunel and launched in 1843, is restored at the Great Western Dock, Bristol. The clipper *Cutty Sark*, launched in 1869, is preserved in its own dock at Greenwich. There are so many other later nineteenth- and twentieth-century British vessels that survive that it is difficult to make a choice. However, the Royal Research Ship *Discovery*, built in 1901 and used by Captain Scott for his Antarctic exploration, is well worth a visit at the Victoria Dock, Dundee; and on an entirely different scale is the unique collection of old steam- and motor-powered boats preserved at the Windermere Steamboat Museum, Windermere.

There have been major efforts to preserve twentieth-century local vessels in Britain, and some have been kept fully restored and in working order. A visit to, say, the Maldon area of Essex will show beautifully restored Thames barges and, with luck, it may be possible to see some in use, with their red sails catching the wind. Elsewhere other vessels are being preserved but not necessarily with full restoration because it is important to retain the evidence of the original vessel, as has happened to the last Rye barge *Primrose*, built about 1890 but with a design and rig that has hardly been changed in four centuries. It was rescued from a river bank near Rye and is preserved at the Shipwreck Heritage Centre, Hastings.

Important examples of twentieth-century ships are also preserved, and several locations are well worth visiting. One is HMS *Belfast* which took part in World War II and is now moored in the River Thames near Tower Bridge; and another is the Submarine Museum and HMS *Alliance*, at Gosport, which preserves the Royal Navy's first submarine known as *Holland I*, which was raised from the seabed in 1982. Mention must also be made of the historic ships collection of the Maritime Trust. This was based at St Katharine's Dock in London until about 1985, but has since been dispersed to locations elsewhere in Britain. These vessels, like the *Kathleen and May*, a late nineteenth-century West Country topsail schooner which is preserved in St Mary Overie Dock, Southwark, close to London Bridge, can be visited by the public, but it is wise to contact the Trust at its London office in advance for details of current locations.

The three great national museums that preserve maritime objects must be mentioned: the National Maritime Museum and the Science Museum in London, and the Merseyside Maritime Museum which is situated in the heart of Liverpool's historic docklands. Also, Chatham Historic Dockyard contains important Naval buildings as well as reused timbers from many 'wooden wall' warships particularly of the nineteenth century which, together with its own exhibition, cannot be missed. An important part of that exhibition is the collection of historic lifeboats. The nearby Guildhall Museum in Rochester also has a maritime collection, as have so many local museums in Britain, and its display is particularly noteworthy.

Further reading

There are many books and other publications on the history of ships, seafaring, maritime trade and warfare, but as important recent archaeological discoveries are increasing our understanding of what sixteenth-century and earlier vessels were like, and how they were built and used, it is necessary to read the latest publications. For later ships the archaeological remains are giving a greater understanding of matters that are otherwise only known from documentary and pictorial sources. Rather than give a long list of publications it would be more useful to give some of the latest important publications on ships and shipwrecks in British waters for in those will be found references to many other significant publications.

In addition to the selected books listed below there are many archaeological reports which appear in the *International Journal of Nautical Archaeology*, published by Academic Press, London, which may be purchased through the Nautical Archaeology Society. Other maritime studies, particularly historical, are published in the *Mariner's Mirror*, which is the Journal of the Society for Nautical Research. Both journals also include reviews of new books on maritime history and archaeology.

Prehistoric, Roman and Saxon

Christensen, A. E. (ed.), *The Earliest Ships: The Evolution of Boats into Ships*, Conway Maritime Press, 1994.

Fenwick, V. (ed.), *The Graveney Boat*, British Archaeological Reports, British Series, 53, 1978.

McGrail, S., *The Ship: Rafts, Boats and Ships from Prehistoric Times to the Medieval Era*, HMSO, 1981.

McGrail, S., *Ancient Boats*, Shire Archaeology, 1983.

McGrail, S., *Ancient Boats in N.W. Europe*, Longman, 1987.

McGrail, S. (ed.), *Maritime Celts, Frisians and Saxons*, CBA Research Report, 71, 1990.

McGrail, S., *Medieval Boat and Ship Timbers from Dublin*, Royal Irish Academy, Dublin, 1993.

Marsden, P., *Ships of the Port of London, First to Eleventh Centuries AD*, English Heritage, 1994.

Rule, M. and Monaghan, J., *A Gallo-Roman Trading Vessel from Guernsey*, Guernsey Museum Monograph, 5, 1993.

Wright, E., *The Ferriby Boats, Seacraft of the Bronze Age*, Routledge, 1990.

Medieval

Gardiner, R. (ed.), *Cogs, Caravels and Galleons: The Sailing Ship 1000–1650*, Conway Maritime Press, 1994.

Hutchinson, G., *Medieval Ships and Shipping*, Leicester University Press, 1994.

Marsden, P., *Ships of the Port of London, Twelfth to Seventeenth Centuries AD*, English Heritage, 1995.

Sixteenth century

Martin, C., *Full Fathom Five: Wrecks of the Spanish Armada*, Chatto & Windus, 1975.

Redknap, M., *The Cattewater Wreck: The Investigation of an Armed Vessel of the Early Sixteenth Century*, British Archaeological Reports, British Series, 131, 1984.

Rule, M., *The Mary Rose: The Excavation and Raising of Henry VIII's Flagship*, Windward, 1983.

Seventeenth to early nineteenth century

Bosscher, P. (ed.), *The Heyday of Sail: The Merchant Sailing Ship 1650–1830*, Conway Maritime Press, 1995.

Gardiner, R. (ed.), *The Line of Battle: The Sailing Warship 1650–1840*, Conway Maritime Press, 1992.

Lavery, B., *The Ship of the Line*. Vol. I. *The Development of the Battlefleet 1650–1850*, Conway Maritime Press, 1983.

Lavery, B., *The Ship of the Line*. Vol. II. *Design, Construction and Fittings*, Conway Maritime Press, 1984.

Lavery, B., *The Royal Navy's First Invincible, 1744–1758: The ship, the Wreck, and the Recovery*, Invincible Conservations (1744–1758) Ltd., 1988.

Marsden, P., *The Wreck of the Amsterdam*, Hutchinson, 1985.

From wood to iron and sail to steam

Gardiner, R. (ed.), *Steam, Steel and Shellfire: The Steam Warship 1815–1905*, Conway Maritime Press, 1992.

Gardiner, R. (ed.), *The Eclipse of the Big Gun: The Warship 1906–1945*, Conway Maritime Press, 1992.

Gardiner, R. (ed.), *The Advent of Steam: The Merchant Steamship Before 1900*, Conway Maritime Press, 1993.

Gardiner, R. (ed.), *Sail's Last Century: The Merchant Sailing Ship 1830–1930*, Conway Maritime Press, 1993.

Greenhill, B., *The Ship: The Life and Death of the Merchant Sailing Ship 1815–1965*, HMSO, 1980.

Lyon, D., *The Ship: Steam, Steel and Torpedoes: The Warship in the 19th Century*, HMSO, 1980.

General archaeological maritime studies

Bass, G. (ed.), *Ships and Shipwrecks of the Americas*, Thames & Hudson, 1996.

Muckleroy, K., *Archaeology Under Water: An Atlas of the World's Submerged Sites*, McGraw-Hill Book Co., 1980.

Throckmorton, P. (ed.), *History from the Sea*, Mitchell Beazley, 1987.

Ports and dockyards

Coad, J., *The Royal Dockyards 1690–1850*, RCHME, 1989.

Ellmers, C. and Werner, A., *Dockland Life: A Pictorial History of London's Docks 1860–1970*, Mainstream Publishing (Edinburgh) Ltd., 1991.

Jackson, G., *The History and Archaeology of Ports*, World's Work Ltd., 1983.

Philp, B., *The Excavation of the Roman Forts of the Classis Britannica at Dover 1970–1977*, Kent Archaeological Rescue Unit, Dover, 1981.

Steedman, K., Dyson, T. and Schofield, J., *Aspects of Saxo-Norman London III: The Bridghead and Billingsgate to 1200*, London and Middlesex Archaeological Society Special Paper, 14, 1992.

Methods of maritime archaeology

Dean, M. *et al.*, *Archaeology Underwater, the NAS guide to Principles and Practice*, Nautical Archaeology Society, London, 1992.

Richard Steffy, J., *Wooden Ship Building and the Interpretation of Shipwrecks*, Texas A&M University Press, 1994.

Understanding ancient ships

Since a ship is a machine it is important to understand how a vessel floats, what makes it stable, how it is propelled and steered, and how its construction can make it strong and safe. The book McGrail 1987, mentioned above, deals with all of these points in relation to ancient vessels, though it is necessary to have some prior knowledge of the subject. The following books will be helpful:

Greenhill, B., *Archaeology of the Boat*, Adam & Charles Black, 1976.

Leather, J., *Clinker Boatbuilding*, Adlard Coles, 1973.

McKee, E., *Working Boats of Britain*, Conway Maritime Press, 1983.

Marchaj, C., *Seaworthiness the Forgotten Factor*, Adlard Coles, 1986.

Simpson, A., *Nautical Knowledge for Fishermen*, Brown, Son & Ferguson, 1979.

Index

(Page numbers in **bold** refer to illustrations.
Dates on their own after the name of a
vessel refer to the date it was sunk.)

The Author

Dr Peter Marsden is Director of the Ships Heritage Centre in Hastings. He was formerly a Senior Archaeologist at the Museum of London and was the City of London Archaeologist in the 1960s. He has a particular interest in shipwrecks having discovered two Roman shipwrecks in London. He is a Fellow of the Society of Antiquaries and did his doctorate in maritime archaeology at Oxford. His hobby is family history.

'One of the great classic series of British archaeology.' *Current Archaeology*